but if not

Finding God in
Unmet Expectations
and Unwanted Detours

CAMILLE FRONK OLSON

DESERET
BOOK

For Jayne

Interior image: Dimitri Otis / Getty Images

© 2025 Camille Fronk Olson

All rights reserved. No part of this book may be reproduced in any form or by any means without permission in writing from the publisher, Deseret Book Company, at permissions@deseretbook.com. This work is not an official publication of The Church of Jesus Christ of Latter-day Saints. The views expressed herein are the responsibility of the author and do not necessarily represent the position of the Church or of Deseret Book Company.

DESERET BOOK is a registered trademark of Deseret Book Company.

Visit us at deseretbook.com

Library of Congress Cataloging-in-Publication Data
(CIP data on file)
ISBN 978-1-63993-423-2

Printed in the United States of America

1 2 3 4 5 LBC 29 28 27 26 25

Contents

CHAPTER ONE:
Unexpected Roadblocks | 1

CHAPTER TWO:
Unfounded Interpretations of the Gospel | 13

CHAPTER THREE:
Opposition in All Things | 41

CHAPTER FOUR:
Our Bodies Are Mortal | 59

CHAPTER FIVE:
Agency vs. Expectations | 73

CHAPTER SIX:
Divinely Designed Paths | 93

CHAPTER SEVEN:
Our Response to the Unexpected | 107

NOTES | 120

CHAPTER ONE

Unexpected Roadblocks

1

Life rarely turns out the way we plan.

We end up in places, going in different directions, and using skills and talents that we never envisioned. We experience unfathomable pain and loss along the way. Each one of us has a personal story to verify that we are no strangers to unmet expectations.

On the eve of my high school graduation, some friends and I sat down to prognosticate our futures. We thought that seeing through the next ten years would pretty much describe the rest of our lives. Considering each of us one by one, we guessed the number of years before marriage, professions of our husbands, the number of children each of us would have, and the distance from our hometown we would live to raise our families. Then I wrote down an additional handful of expectations for me, including skills I would master and ways I would make a difference in society in the future. After ten years elapsed, not one of my expectations had materialized. It would be closer to thirty years before anything on my list occurred, with the great majority of my expectations unfulfilled.

Most of our expectations as teenagers focused on skills and roles that we discussed in our church mutual classes. In our minds, these goals were exactly what God wanted for each of His daughters and we were happy to fulfill His dreams for us. But the unexpected happened and our lives took different turns than we foresaw. For three in our group, serious diseases shortened their lives, for another infidelity ended her marriage, another adopted her children because of infertility, another suffered significant financial loss, another bore a child with disabilities, another watched her children leave the religion she loved, and I didn't even get a marriage proposal, let alone marry. Was there something wrong with what we expected and planned for in life?

In a world where we encounter previously unknown circumstances almost routinely, when we constantly hear of events being "unprecedented," we wonder what tomorrow will bring and how to plan for an uncertain future. New inventions, technology, legislation, career opportunities, political plots, wars, virus strains, and natural disasters

UNEXPECTED ROADBLOCKS

invade our carefully designed plans for a happy and contributing life.

Layered on top of these societal shifts are personal unexpected occurrences that can make it feel like our world has suddenly turned sideways. A debilitating accident, domestic abuse, the premature death of a loved one, an incurable health diagnosis, a family member's disavowal of their faith tradition, gender identity confusion, inability to bear children, singleness, job severance, unfair legal verdicts, mental illness, and the list goes on. No one can plan for all the possible setbacks that could occur to any of us at any time. That is why any attempt to keep tight control of our lives, so they run smoothly and are void of pain and drama, is soon dashed.

Furthermore, none of us travels the exact same path through mortality. When President Russell M. Nelson and others remind us to stay on the covenant path, I don't think they envision one universal way to go through life in lockstep rhythm with everyone else. That covenant path contains the same essential covenants and ordinances for all, but the shape, length, and circuitousness of

> That covenant path contains the same essential covenants and ordinances for all, but the shape, length, and circuitousness of the path differ for each one of us.

the path differ for each one of us. Each of us has a unique story with ups and downs, even cavernous downs, yet the ultimate destination on the path can be the same because of the mercy and grace of Jesus Christ.

Psychologists have posited that unfulfilled expectations are one of the greatest causes of unhappiness, making expectations of any kind potentially hazardous. One article reports, "Happiness is usually proportional to our level of acceptance [of the way our lives turn out] and inversely proportional to our expectations." Rather than jettison all our dreams for the future and expect doom and gloom in their place, the article continues by underscoring an important purpose that expectations can perform, "The main function of expectations is to prepare for action. If we mentally anticipate what may happen, we can prepare an action plan so that life does not take us by surprise. Expectations, therefore, help us prepare mentally for the future."[1] Even though our life's plans need to be continually reworked along the way, the fact that we have a plan propels us to act and be ready to pivot and refocus when unforeseen events become roadblocks in our path.

What happens, however, when our expectations are tied to promised blessings in the restored gospel of Jesus Christ and yet evade fulfillment? Despite our diligence and obedience to God, we may find our path is no longer

UNEXPECTED ROADBLOCKS

passable, our strength is not sufficient to enable us to continue, or we reach the door at the top of the incline only to find it is closed and locked. When a disconnect occurs between what we believe God promises and what we receive, our happiness level can plummet while our disillusionment with divine dictates can mushroom exponentially. How can we understand the gap between our expectations and our reality through the lens of the restored gospel? Did God block my way on the path and if so, why? Did I misunderstand the directions and therefore take a wrong turn? Did someone choose to close the door and shut me out? Can they do that? Does God allow that? Or did some natural phenomena damage the path and impede my progression? If I do my part, isn't God bound to give me my righteous desires?

This little book consists of teachings from multiple sources that I have explored and pondered, experimented on and analyzed, while studying and teaching the gospel of Jesus Christ in the face of heartache, sleepless nights, and unmet expectations in my life. I don't pretend to understand and have specific answers for the myriads of ways lives are uprooted, hoisted in the air, and dropped in foreign territory. But I know and trust the word of God, His plan of happiness, and His healing balm.

Like Meshach, Shadrach, and Abed-nego said when

they were about to be thrown into a fiery furnace because they would not bow down and worship the graven image of King Nebuchadnezzar, "If it be so [that you throw us into the furnace], our God . . . will deliver us out of thine hand, O king. *But if not,* . . . we will not serve thy gods, nor worship the golden image which thou hast set up" (Daniel 3:17–18; emphasis added). Their trust in their God was fully grounded in their humble awareness that God knew more than they did and whatever He did would be for their benefit. It was not dependent on mortal outcomes. It was not conditioned on God's response to *their* desires. Their response to a very bad situation underscores true faith in the Lord. *But if not.* Can my faith be equally unshakable? When the outcome doesn't materialize as I expect, can I be like Meshach, Shadrach, and Abed-nego and not forsake Him?

My hope is that, through all the unwanted detours life throws at us, we come to know our Savior better and hear His voice more distinctly. Amid times of uncertainty, when we hear Him, we may then more wisely embrace unforeseen opportunities that invite us to mature in wisdom and develop more of His attributes. In multiple

> In multiple ways and for multiple reasons, life rarely turns out the way we expect—and maybe, just maybe, that's a good thing.

ways and for multiple reasons, life rarely turns out the way we expect—and maybe, just maybe, that's a good thing.

In each of the following five chapters, I explore a different category for why our expectations to personally live our life in Christ are so often unmet. I don't see these categories as distinct and mutually exclusive. One overlaps and blurs into another. Furthermore, I don't think we can often assign one specific category to explain the reason for a particular disruption. But sometimes we might. Much of the value comes in sensing God's presence and awareness, whatever the reason and circumstance. His presence does not justify those who knowingly upset our plans, but it gives us hope that He will still show us the Way forward.

Chapter 2 deals with unmet expectations that are based on uninformed or inaccurate interpretations of God's promises. What if we misunderstand the doctrine and assume connections that are not part of His plan of happiness? I will discuss examples of scriptures that, when taken out of context, can lead to very different and even inaccurate explanations for divine promises than intended.

This is a very different explanation for unfulfilled expectations from what I discuss in chapters 3 through 5, which consider the consequences of living in a fallen world. From the beginning, God blessed Adam and Eve with circumstances laced with pain and suffering that they might learn through opposition in all things. By extension, we too may learn to become like our Savior through our own encounters with opposition. Chapter 3 explores the value of such opposition and some ways it can inform our expectations. Chapter 4 reminds us of the natural laws that govern our world, particularly as our mortal bodies respond to them. Chapter 5 considers the role agency, which God grants to each of His children, plays in derailing many of our dreams for the future.

Chapter 6 investigates still another reason why an expected path may be blocked. This category prefigures an omniscient and omnipotent Father who sees a mission for each of us and will steer us to it. This divine design is often a path we never imagined, let alone expected, that can dramatically change the details and mortal trajectory of our lives.

> This divine design is often a path we never imagined, let alone expected.

The concluding chapter explores how we respond to disrupted hopes in life, and why the way we respond may matter far more than the details of what eventually transpires.

Throughout each chapter of the book, however, I hope

UNEXPECTED ROADBLOCKS

that you, the reader, will sincerely contemplate whether unmet expectations can be transformed into a precious gift—a gift that offers far more than we could have ever imagined.

CHAPTER TWO

Unfounded Interpretations of the Gospel

2

I remember hearing about a member of the Church living in Russia who reads the Book of Mormon every year so that he won't be surprised when bad things happen to good people. The truth is, you can look at any book of scripture and any era of history and find the same reality; bad things are always happening to good people, including you and me. Right? So why does it surprise us? Where is it recorded in scripture that God promises a life void of strife and unpleasant surprises if we love and obey Him? Where is it taught that by keeping the commandments of God, we are ensured that our prayers are answered at the time and in the way we request? Therefore, why do we lose faith and blame God when that doesn't happen?

In His infinite wisdom and grace, God enacted divine laws that indeed confirm blessings to those who exercise faith in Jesus Christ and are willing to live His gospel.

BUT IF NOT

Previous prophets recorded these promises in scripture and living prophets proclaim them from the pulpit. How do we interpret the timing, circumstances, and nature of these promised blessings? I wonder how many faithful Christians have walked away from religion because of an inaccurate understanding of divine laws, which led to unrealistic expectations that never materialized. So, we might ask ourselves, are my unmet expectations based on a faulty interpretation of God's plan of happiness?

Here's a scriptural example of a young man's deep disappointment that resulted from misunderstanding the Lord's teachings. The synoptic gospels recount the story of a rich young ruler[1] who came to the Savior with a question. In the Mark account, the young man ran to greet Jesus, then, showing deep reverence, knelt before Him to ask his question. "Good Master," he petitioned, "what shall I do that I may inherit eternal life?" (Mark 10:17; see also Luke 18:18). The Matthew account adds interesting clues about what the young man expected in the Savior's answer. He first asked, "What *good thing* shall I do, that I may have eternal life?" (Matthew 19:16; emphasis added). Notice that he expected the answer to contain only one doing, one action, one "good thing" needed to gain eternal life. When Jesus taught, "If thou wilt enter into life, keep the commandments," the young man quickly asked Him for

UNFOUNDED INTERPRETATIONS OF THE GOSPEL

clarification: "Which?" (Matthew 19:17–18). I can almost picture him with the ancient equivalent of a tiny notepad and pen, ready to jot down a small, concluding, ancillary task he needed to perform to earn eternal life. In his mind, he could see the finish line. Just a bit of final polishing yet to do.

Consequently, the young disciple might have been a bit impatient listening to the Savior's next instruction. Jesus began listing many of the known commandments: don't steal, don't kill, don't lie, honor your parents. I can imagine that young man thinking, "Yes, yes, yes. I know all that. That isn't what I'm asking." What he answered aloud was, "All these things have I kept from my youth up: what lack I yet?" (Matthew 19:20). Clearly, this was a good young man. He caused no trouble in society and probably did much good. But his was a checklist mentality. He saw the commandments as tasks to be "completed" in short order rather than a process and lifelong endeavor to assist us in becoming more like our Savior. The full context of the Matthew account begs us to consider holes in the young man's gospel understanding and how he might experience a more profound level of discipleship with Jesus Christ by opening his mind and heart to discover the Lord's *abundant* gospel. A gospel that enables us to do, understand, and become more—much more—over time.

BUT IF NOT

Considering his comprehension of the gospel at the time, how would the rich young ruler understand "obedience" to the Lord's commandments? He was young and had wealth, power, and status in his community. Although we don't know his parents, the implication is that they were well-to-do and gave their son every possible opportunity to excel. This young man's identity was likely established on status and wealth rather than losing oneself in discipleship with Christ. Does obedience appear differently to someone who owns everything that society values than it does to those who experience loss and hardship daily? What does the command to not steal mean to someone who has "great possessions"? How does the commandment change when you have no material comforts, possessions, or security, or when you don't know where your next meal will come from? How challenging is it to not covet when you already own what everyone else wants? And how would the difficulty of obedience to the commandment to honor parents be altered when those parents are not supportive or are even destructive to our heartfelt aspirations?

When the Savior invited the rich young ruler to be challenged and discover a deeper commitment to obey God in all things, He said, "If thou wilt be perfect [or complete, whole], go and sell what thou hast, and give to the poor, and thou shalt have treasure in heaven: and come and follow me" (Matthew 19:21). In other words, Jesus was asking him to learn obedience through hardship and the trial of his faith, as He, our Savior, learned it: "Yet learned he obedience by the things which he suffered" (Hebrews 5:8).

By giving all his possessions to the poor and committing his life to support the Savior in His travels and mission, this young man was poised to learn and experience an entirely new level of understanding of what he could become through fellowship with the Lord. I don't think this incident is meant to communicate that wealthy people cannot become true disciples of Christ, but to teach how privilege and possessions can define us and consequently threaten or thwart our spiritual progression by making it easier to misinterpret the Lord's commands. If the young man relinquished his accustomed life of luxury, even for a brief time, he could be better prepared to recognize an inherent cost of true discipleship with Jesus Christ—that it isn't a simple checklist of tasks to be completed. This change in perspective could then educate him to a deeper understanding of the power, inspiration, and joy that can come from "keeping" or safeguarding the commandments.

I like to connect the Savior's answer to this young man about obtaining eternal life to one that Nephi gave in the Book of Mormon. Nephi articulated a lifetime process to finally receive "the greatest of all the gifts of God" (Doctrine and Covenants 14:7) when he wrote, "Ye must *press forward* with a steadfastness in Christ, having a perfect brightness of hope, and a love of God and of all men. Wherefore, if ye shall *press forward*, feasting upon the word of Christ, and *endure to the end*, behold, thus saith the Father: Ye shall have eternal life" (2 Nephi 31:20; emphasis added). Had the rich young ruler learned about obtaining eternal life from Nephi, he would have heard something more than an easy checklist in the counsel Jesus gave to him.

When we next see this young man in the story, he is walking away "sorrowful: for he had great possessions" (Matthew 19:22). We observe that his expectation of being praised for his goodness was not realized—because of an unfounded and simplistic understanding of what discipleship with Jesus Christ entails. Our hearts break for him, for what he could become, and for what he doesn't yet comprehend.

A well-known and oft-repeated promise in the Book of Mormon, if taken out of context, can lead to a faulty interpretation of this doctrine, just as the rich young ruler experienced. The familiar passage is, "Inasmuch as ye shall keep my commandments ye shall prosper in the land; but inasmuch as ye will not keep my commandments ye shall be cut off from my presence" (2 Nephi 1:20). Without

UNFOUNDED INTERPRETATIONS OF THE GOSPEL

any context or accompanying examples in the Book of Mormon, it is natural to conclude that God is promising a life of ease and material wealth if we will simply keep His commandments, in whatever naïve way we may choose to define "keeping" the commandments.

How did Book of Mormon prophets understand God's promise of prosperity? Does it agree with the way that today's society uses the term? A strain of modern Christianity, often called "the prosperity gospel,"[2] subscribes to this faulty interpretation. It claims that God rewards the faithful with wealth, health, and happiness in response to their positive declarations and financial donations to religious causes. Financial success and physical well-being are then seen as evidence of righteousness and receipt of God's favor. According to this false explanation of the gospel, lack of health and wealth advertises a believer's failure to receive God's approval.

Neither writers of the Bible, nor Book of Mormon authors, nor our own life experiences witness that this interpretation is correct. What did Nephi and others mean when they testified that God promised prosperity to those who kept His commandments? Seeing the promise as an "if this, then that" couplet holds the strongest hint for defining "prosper" according to Book of Mormon prophets. Look at it as a set of opposing conditions. If a specific condition (A) holds, then a specific outcome (B) occurs; and if the opposite of that condition (-A) holds, then the opposite outcome (-B) will result. The first phrase in the second line is clearly the exact opposite of the first phrase in the first line:

> A = Inasmuch as ye shall keep my commandments . . .
> -A = Inasmuch as ye will NOT keep my commandments . . .

Therefore, the second phrase of each line should also constitute a set of opposites:

> B = . . . Ye shall prosper in the land.
> -B = . . . Ye shall be cut off from my presence.

Looking at it as a mathematical structure, what then is the opposite of prospering in the land? Being cut off from God's presence. Therefore, what does it mean to "prosper in the land"? NOT being cut off from God's presence.

Having the Lord's presence in our daily life through the companionship of the Holy Ghost is the promise the Lord gives to all those who sincerely strive to remember Him and keep His commandments. We hear this correlation between obedience and receiving the Spirit every single week in the sacrament prayers when we renew our covenants with God. Getting rich and staying physically robust is not included in the promise. After all, do we all know of some exceedingly wealthy people and some incredibly gifted athletes who care nothing about God and His commandments? Whereas those who reverence the Lord and His gospel can be found all along the economic continuum. "Render therefore unto Caesar the things which are Caesar's," the Lord declared while looking at a coin engraved with Caesar's image, "and unto God the things that are God's" (Matthew 22:21). God doesn't value monetary status; He values each of us, those created in His image. His sons and His daughters. Our hearts, our minds, our souls. Our mortal bodies may be challenged in every way, yet we can still feel His presence and learn from Him. His greatest gift to us in mortality is His Spirit as a companion to teach, direct, warn, and correct us each day of our lives. This invaluable gift in turn empowers us to make better decisions and learn from previous missteps.

> God doesn't value monetary status; He values each of us, those created in His image. His sons and His daughters.

I invite you to look at the context of what is happening in the Book of Mormon narrative every time you encounter this set of opposites. Admittedly, in some instances, the people are blessed with material prosperity when they "prosper," but not always. The absence of material wealth and physical well-being in most cases suggests that health and wealth are not explicit conditions of prosperity. In every context that the term shows up in the Book of Mormon, however, the people are blessed by the presence of the Spirit, who directs and inspires them to have more meaningful lives.

If we get God's promises wrong in this doctrine of the gospel by expecting material increase and physical health, we may conclude that we have failed in God's eyes and that He has rejected us when our expectations aren't fulfilled. Or we may blame God for not keeping His promises. Or stop believing in Him altogether. *But if not . . .* Does our loyalty to the Lord depend on financial worth? Or can we refocus on God's greatest gifts?

Without paying the price of doctrinal study and subsequently applying scriptural teachings to understand the restored gospel, it is easy to buy into cultural expectations and perpetuate them when fulfilling our assignments in the Church. Accepting and disseminating culturally accepted expectations can be very damaging to our own and others' testimonies. Whether we are invited to speak in sacrament meeting, teach a class, or engage in gospel discussions at home, questions arise that we often answer with hearsay, especially if we haven't searched out the answer on our own. When something taught doesn't sound right, it

UNFOUNDED INTERPRETATIONS OF THE GOSPEL

behooves us to search it out by asking clarifying questions, seeking authoritative sources, and praying for guidance. Each of us has a right to the Spirit's tutelage of what is true doctrine and what is not. By striving to increase our gospel understanding with continual study and faith, we will educate our expectations with good doctrine rather than with our own wishes and an escape from our fears.

As children, we need simple approaches to understand the gospel and ignite our faith in Jesus Christ. Those approaches, however, don't always work for adults when life becomes far more complicated. One way we stymie our gospel knowledge and envision unrealistic expectations is by choosing isolated scriptures as our rationale for supporting a self-created theology. Proof-texting (also referred to as "cherry-picking") is when we select comfortable passages without acknowledging the context and without wrestling with what may initially appear as contradicting passages. This shortcut approach to scripture study can set us up for ungrounded and irrational expectations.

For example, a favorite verse for encouraging obedience to God is Doctrine and Covenants 82:10. "I, the Lord, am bound when ye do what I say; but when ye do not what I say, ye have no promise." We may conclude from this verse that if I don't shop on the Sabbath and I pay my tithing, etc., etc., He promises to grant me what I need and desire. Given this interpretation, when someone is killed in an accident, should we conclude that they or their family broke a commandment for which they are being punished? When my loved one rejects her faith, did I do something wrong? If I cling to the assumption that my prayers for safety will ensure no accident ever befalls me or my loved ones, and my family's testimonies will always remain intact, how do I perceive my Father in Heaven when disappointment isn't averted? When no external evidence magically appears to provide proof of the historicity of the Book of Mormon, the divine prophetic calling of Joseph Smith, or the fact that God chooses faithful though imperfect disciples to lead His Church, do we conclude revelation is a myth? Elder D. Todd Christofferson explained, "It is essential that we honor and obey His laws, but *not every blessing predicated on obedience to law is shaped, designed, and timed according to our expectations.* We do our best but must leave to Him the management of blessings, both temporal and spiritual."[3]

Without deeper thinking and searching, by ignoring Elder Christofferson's wisdom and praying a singsong list of requests and routine platitudes, we can inadvertently misinterpret this scriptural promise to re-create God into something akin to a candy dispenser: I want this blessing, so

UNFOUNDED INTERPRETATIONS OF THE GOSPEL

I insert this act of obedience, push the button, and *voila!* the blessing is dispensed. *But if not* . . . how will we respond?

Elder Christofferson warned us to beware of such simplistic reasoning:

> Some misunderstand the promises of God to mean that obedience to Him yields specific outcomes on a fixed schedule. They might think, "If I diligently serve a full-time mission, God will bless me with a happy marriage and children" or "If I refrain from doing schoolwork on the Sabbath, God will bless me with good grades" or "If I pay tithing, God will bless me with that job I've been wanting." If life doesn't fall out precisely this way or according to an expected timetable, they may feel betrayed by God. But things are not so mechanical in the divine economy. We ought not to think of God's plan as a cosmic vending machine where we (1) select a desired blessing, (2) insert the required sum of good works, and (3) the order is promptly delivered.[4]

What Elder Christofferson is describing is the gospel of positive thinking: If you can conceive of an outcome, you can pray it into fruition. It's another version of the prosperity gospel. This belief works—until it doesn't.

And each of us has a firsthand example of when it hasn't worked.

Instead of interpreting the verse in the way we want it to mean, we may try finding connections between Doctrine and Covenants 82:10 and related (and sometimes seemingly contradicting) scriptures and stories for added explanation, like Mosiah 7:33 in the Book of Mormon. Here is the brief context of this verse. After poor judgment and hubris led a group of Nephites into being in bondage to the Lamanites, the Nephites repented and turned to God in fervent prayer to deliver them. After an uncomfortable period of time in which the reader expects divine deliverance for this remorseful people, their leader, King Limhi, taught what he had learned about receiving answers from God: "But if you will turn to the Lord with full purpose of heart, and put your trust in him, and serve him with all diligence of mind, if you do this, he will, according to his own will and pleasure, deliver you out of bondage" (Mosiah 7:33). Rather than contradicting Doctrine and Covenants 82:10, this stunning verse teases out a deeper understanding about how the Lord answers our efforts to "do what [He] say[s]."

First, Limhi instructs us to turn to the Lord "with full purpose of heart." To me, that means that I plead to God in faith, knowing He is the only one who can deliver me in my distress. My prayers acknowledge that truth because they come from my whole soul.

Next, Limhi taught that we are to put our trust in the Lord. To me, that indicates that perhaps my full-purpose-of-heart prayers weren't answered as quickly as I expected. *But if not* . . . I will not abandon my faith in Him. He continues to be my only hope for deliverance. I will stay true to Him for however long the bondage or challenge will last, whether deliverance comes in this life or the next. In recounting the story, Mormon repeats the phrase "and it came to pass" often. In other words, time passes—sometimes even a long, long time—yet Limhi's people and each of us can still be found turned to the Lord no matter what else may or may not happen.

In the meantime, Limhi didn't say that we are to just hang out and wait until the Lord sees fit to rescue us; he directed us to "serve [God] with all diligence of mind" while yet in bondage. In essence, we need to be up and doing, reaching out to others in love. Although suffering ourselves, we ease our pain by recognizing that others are also struggling and by seeking ways to comfort them. In so doing, we may be the means the Lord uses to deliver another valiant soul who has been pleading to God for deliverance.

Rather than asking the questions "Why is this happening to us?" or "Has God forgotten us?" Limhi directed his people to exercise their faith in Jesus Christ over the long haul, seeking ways to lighten another's burden, discovering evidence that God was with them, and witnessing strengths in themselves that they had not known before. Does Limhi's teaching help you find deeper insight and even greater power in the Lord's promise when we do what He says? Taken together, these verses can better inform the rich young ruler's question for Jesus. We begin to comprehend the power, wisdom, and beauty of the Lord's law of obedience.

Here's another example. One of the first passages of scripture young Latter-day Saints learn is James 1:5. "If any of you lack wisdom, let him ask of God, that giveth to all men liberally, and upbraideth not; and it shall be given him." Taking it out of context and relying solely on young Joseph Smith's experience of learning which church to join, we could expect divine answers to come quickly, directly, and spectacularly. Such a conclusion, however, was not what James was teaching in his epistle. He wanted his audience to recognize that it isn't enough to simply ask God for answers but instead enjoined us to grow our steadfast belief in our omniscient and omnipotent Father to influence our actions. Our beliefs and actions are then in harmony and will strengthen each other. God doesn't simply give answers to satisfy our curiosity. He gives us answers that invite us *to act* on what He just taught us. In other words, young Joseph exemplified his trust in God when he asked for direction, but the divine response he received in the grove was only the beginning of the Father and Son's response to the boy. Joseph needed then to act on what he'd learned through faith. Over time, he was led line upon line, day after day, year after year, to eventually restore the gospel of Jesus Christ to the earth. When we acknowledge that to "ask of God," according to James, is the "faith" part, and putting into action what we learn from God is the "works" part, we connect our isolated verse to the overarching theme of James's epistle: "Faith without works is dead" (James 2:20).

If we identify the context of the epistle, we can then appreciate the relevance of the verses that immediately precede James 1:5. In these opening verses, James acknowledges that we are encompassed by multiple temptations that try our faith in God and, in turn, allow us to learn patience. He then instructed, "But let patience have her perfect work, that ye may be perfect [or whole, complete] and entire, wanting nothing. If any of you lack wisdom, let him ask of God" (James 1:4–5). When taken together, these verses contribute a stunning addition to our understanding about a prayer of faith. Often, God does not answer our prayers in the exact manner and within the time we desire—which requires patience on our part. It might happen over a longer period than we anticipate. *But if not.* "Let patience have her perfect work." Patience requires time—lots of time—to complete its purpose. Patience is not interested in efficiency and instant returns. Patience grows in power and wisdom over long stretches of time and uncertainty. James tells us (including young Joseph Smith) that if we are lacking wisdom, we probably aren't going to receive it overnight. We may receive direction for the next step in our journey, but only God sees the full terrain ahead, including dead ends, staggering inclines, precarious cliffs, and stunning vistas.

President Susan H. Porter testified that fervent prayer often requires patience when she told of praying as a Primary child that her father would be baptized and take her family to the temple. She was still offering that heartfelt prayer when she was a grandmother. Five days after

UNFOUNDED INTERPRETATIONS OF THE GOSPEL

her eighty-six-year-old father passed away, she related, "Heavenly Father let me know through His Spirit that my father wanted to receive the blessings of the gospel of Jesus Christ!"[5] Patience requires time to work miracles.

Discipleship means that we not only retain but increase our faith and trust in Him, growing in understanding each step of the way as we manifest that faith by our actions. As the Lord instructed Oliver Cowdery, "Be *patient,* my son, for it is *wisdom in me.* . . . You have not understood; you have supposed that I would give it unto you, when you took no thought *save it was to ask me*" (Doctrine and Covenants 9:3, 7; emphasis added). The Lord is the source of all wisdom; wisdom is *in Him.* To gain wisdom ourselves requires us to ask Him in faith, continually and sincerely, and let patience have her perfect work. I believe the life of Joseph Smith bears witness to that truth.

Long ago I heard a quote from President Spencer W. Kimball that comes to mind when I complain, "Why is this happening to me?" and "This life isn't fair." President Kimball taught:

> Some become bitter when oft-repeated prayers seem unanswered. . . . But if all the sick were healed, if all the righteous were protected and the wicked destroyed, the whole program of the Father

would be annulled and the basic principle of the gospel, free agency, would be ended.... If pain and sorrow and total punishment immediately followed the doing of evil, no soul would repeat a misdeed. If joy and peace and rewards were instantaneously given the doer of good, there could be no evil—all would do good and not because of the rightness of doing good. There would be no test of strength, no development of character, no growth of powers, no free agency.... There would also be an absence of joy, success, resurrection, eternal life, and godhood.[6]

The Father's glorious plan of happiness demands a more robust theology and doctrinal foundation than what we learned as children in Primary. Our home-centered scripture studies for *Come, Follow Me* are given not as a nice suggestion but for our spiritual survival. There is no substitute for consistent, inquisitive, and prayerful study of the word of God.

> There is no substitute for consistent, inquisitive, and prayerful study of the word of God.

Elder Neal A. Maxwell of the Quorum of the Twelve Apostles spoke of challenging doctrines that are important aspects of the restored gospel. He taught, "There are

UNFOUNDED INTERPRETATIONS OF THE GOSPEL

in the gospel warm and cuddly doctrines, and then there are some that are just outright *wintry* doctrines. . . . We avert our gaze [from the wintry doctrines] because we don't wish to contemplate them."[7] Expanding our understanding of the gospel to include the "wintry doctrines," as Elder Maxwell called them, will lead to more realistic expectations. If we don't progress in our doctrinal understanding, we are bound to be disappointed at best and angry at God at worst. A sincere and consistent gospel study strengthens not only our understanding of doctrine but our trust in God and His Son. We are reminded through countless scriptural examples of believers who endured severe hardships and came out the other side with deeper love for God and those around them, even when the outcome wasn't what they expected. Wintry doctrines carry the capacity to build faith in the Lord and conviction to follow Him in ways impossible by cuddly teachings alone. Times of pain and uncertainty can then show us God's love most clearly when we turn, trust, and serve Him.

Because of avoiding wintry doctrines and misunderstanding God's promises, we may begin to expect perfection from our Church leaders and the Church itself. If we demand perfection, it is easy to conclude that this cannot be the true Church of Jesus Christ when our bishops don't behave as we expect or when fellow members ignore us.

BUT IF NOT

I don't mean to make this sound childish. Some offenses are deeply jarring and disruptive. But do we ever find ourselves expecting more of others in the Church than we do of ourselves? How easy is it to then blame God for choosing imperfect people who are doing their best to serve us?

Considered from a different angle, do unfounded interpretations of our doctrine lead us to forget the reason *we chose* to come to earth? Think about it. Our purpose here is not to prove that we can endure mortality without ever making a mistake. It isn't to show how we can raise a perfect family (whatever that means) or become the most successful expert in our field of work. Aren't we here to learn to become like our Savior? The Apostle Paul called this transformation becoming "joint-heirs with Christ; if [it] so be that we *suffer with him*, that we may be also glorified together" (Romans 8:17; emphasis added). Paul's description of becoming like Jesus Christ suggests that mortality will surprise us with unexpected and steep learning curves.

Building our foundation on the only inexhaustible and enduring Bedrock gives us the opportunity to develop strength to stand when challenges hit.

Remember in Jesus's parable that the rains and floods hit the house built on the rock every bit as much as the one built on sand. Being built on the Rock of our Redeemer didn't prevent the storms of life. Rather, building our foundation on the only inexhaustible and enduring Bedrock gives us the opportunity to develop strength to stand when challenges hit. In fact, Helaman encouraged his sons to build on the Rock of our Redeemer, because *when* (not if) the devil sends "forth his mighty winds" and "his shafts in the whirlwind," if we are built on the only Sure Footing, we "*cannot* fall" (Helaman 5:12; emphasis added). That is because this Bedrock is the "Messiah, the King of Zion, the Rock of Heaven, which is *broad as eternity*; whoso cometh in at the gate and climbeth up by [Him] shall *never* fall" (Moses 7:53; emphasis added).

Elder Dieter F. Uchtdorf explained a further insight from this parable. He wrote, "A house doesn't survive in a storm because the house is strong. It also doesn't survive just because the rock is strong. The house survives the storm because it is firmly attached to that strong rock. It's the strength of the *connection* to the rock that matters."[8] Our relationship with our Father in Heaven and our Savior Jesus Christ holds the power to help us to stand, or get up again, when Satan sends shafts in the whirlwind our way. Therefore, perhaps the Lord's greatest blessing to us in mortality is that He will "prosper" us or give us His presence at all times, and in all places.

BUT IF NOT

Let's return to the rich young ruler. Jesus saw the sincerity and hope in this young man when he reported, "Master, all these have I observed from my youth." At this point in the story, the Mark account adds a tender insight into the Savior: "Then Jesus beholding him loved him" (Mark 10:20–21). In our ignorance of His doctrines, the Lord desires to teach us and grant us understanding and wisdom. He stands ready to welcome us to Him if we turn to Him, trust Him, and serve Him. The fact that He asks more diligence from us is to deepen and broaden our ability to become like Him. Rather than be discouraging, He invites us, "Take my yoke upon you, and learn of me" (Matthew 11:29), while providing a plethora of resources and support to do so.

Did the rich young ruler later open his heart and mind to experiment upon the challenge the Savior issued to him? Did he choose to trust in Him and give up his life of luxury and ease? Sometimes I like to imagine he could be the seemingly random young man wearing nothing but a linen cloth who came upon the suffering Savior in Gethsemane (see Mark 14:51–52). That he later accepted the invitation of Jesus, gave all he had, and committed to follow Him. In truth, we don't know what happened to the rich young ruler. The scriptures are silent on that point. But not on the examples of many who did indeed give up all they had to follow Him. "A religion that does not require the sacrifice of all things," we read in *Lectures on Faith*, "never has power sufficient to produce the faith necessary unto life and salvation."[9]

Unmet expectations that are based on faulty interpretations of God's promises will inevitably result in disappointment. Becoming more conversant in and converted to true doctrine, by contrast, will open doors to greater empathy, fulfillment, and satisfaction. That doesn't happen by studying alone, but by striving to put into practice what we know to be true. In other words, we may become doctrinally savvy, but experientially naïve. Practice, however, involves falling, taking wrong turns, and even suffering pain at times. All our practice will also help us to minister more effectively to others. Along the way, we become less likely to judge, better at listening, and more able to show compassion. Our relationships with others will subsequently grow stronger and our discussions more grounded in glorious gospel truths. All of this builds the foundation for a more satisfying life.

CHAPTER THREE

Opposition in All Things

3

Our mortal experience was created to allow and encourage learning by faith through unfairness, suffering, and opposition. From the beginning, God blessed Adam and Eve with circumstances that allowed them to experience natural consequences from various sources of opposition. That tutelage required leaving the Garden and entering a fallen world.

Remember that the only things God cursed in the Garden were the serpent and the ground. Neither Adam nor Eve was cursed. Far from cursing them, the Eden story cites God blessing both Adam and Eve with "sorrow." This word in Hebrew, `*itstsabown* or *'etseb* (both forms from the root 'tsb),[1] does not suggest circumstances that simply make us sorry, but conditions that are challenging and require great toil, pain, and suffering to work through. Adam was told, "Cursed is the ground *for thy sake;* in sorrow [`itstsabown`] shalt thou eat of it all the days of thy life" (Genesis 3:17; emphasis added; see also Moses 4:23). Hard work is not a curse. It is the catalyst for learning many of life's greatest lessons. God knew that working through uncertainties and hardships is essential to developing character and becoming more like Him. J. Richard Clarke, then a member of the Presiding Bishopric, taught, "Work is honorable. It is good therapy for most problems. It is the antidote for worry. It is the equalizer for deficiency of native endowment. Work makes it possible for the average to approach genius. What we may lack in aptitude, we can make up for in performance."[2] Opportunities to develop a relationship with the Lord and His work were amplified by requiring Adam to work by the sweat of his brow to bring sustenance from the ground.

Parallel to what He declared to Adam, God told Eve, "I will greatly multiply thy sorrow [`itstsabown`] and thy conception; in sorrow [`'etseb`] thou shalt bring forth children" (Genesis 3:16; Moses 4:22). It is easy to conflate Eve's blessing here to refer only to childbearing, thereby suggesting that God is telling Woman that her pain and suffering would occur only in childbirth. A careful reading of the scripture and real-life experience should challenge that quick assumption.

I remember when the silliness of concluding that women's only worries, difficulty, and pain would come from childbirth became apparent. I was a relatively new assistant professor at BYU and along with a colleague was interviewed for a small radio program. Among the questions asked us was one about Adam and Eve. I don't remember the particulars except that my colleague related the Hebrew meaning for "sorrow" and explained that men don't experience the profound pain that women do in childbirth; however, while women's suffering is more intense, it is short-lived (confined solely to childbirth), whereas men's suffering is less intense but stretched out over a lifetime. I was so taken aback by this assumption that I must have audibly guffawed. I remember saying something like, "You're joking, aren't you? If you ask any mother about pain and suffering, they will tell you that the giving-birth part was easy in comparison to the worries and pains she experienced while mothering her children and grandchildren in the decades afterwards." Since then, I've thought of another reason to question his conclusion. What about women who never bear children? Does that mean they go through mortality without any hardships that cause pain and heartache? Of course not.

Ever since that day, I have read this passage as God telling Eve that He would teach her through "sorrow" in two ways. The verse uses the Hebrew word translated "sorrow" twice for Eve, the first in a general context and the second in the context of childbearing. "I will greatly multiply thy sorrow and . . . in sorrow thou shalt bring forth children." She therefore experiences sorrow in two circumstances: "I will greatly multiply thy pain and suffering in life generally, *and* I will also give you hardship in childbirth."

Author Melinda Wheelwright Brown beautifully summarized the blessing of learning through times of sorrow. "Eve and Adam have each had the consequences of their choices realistically described to them; each has been similarly instructed and similarly endowed regarding the challenges that await them. . . . These distinct blessings . . . are for our sake and for our good, providing us with the very struggles that will ultimately refine and transform us."[3] From the moment Adam and Eve left the Garden, they and their posterity would begin to experience the consequences of opposition in all things.

No one is exempt from these opposing forces, not even Jesus during His mortality. "[He] learned . . . obedience by the things which he suffered" (Hebrews 5:8). Moreover, each of us *chose* to come to fallen Earth, recognizing that we would face hardships to know joy and fulfillment. Elder

OPPOSITION IN ALL THINGS

Dieter F. Uchtdorf explained, "Life is not an endless sequence of emotional highs.... And if God Himself weeps, as the scriptures affirm He does, then of course you and I will weep as well. Feeling sad is not a sign of failure. In this life, at least, joy and sorrow are inseparable companions."[4]

Nearly every six months at general conference, at least one of our leaders reminds us of the value of opposition in all things. In 2020, President Jeffrey R. Holland drew on something Elder Neal A. Maxwell said twenty years earlier when he stressed that:

"One's life . . . cannot be both faith-filled and stress-free." It simply will not work to "glide naively through life," saying as we sip another glass of lemonade, "Lord, give me all thy choicest virtues, but be certain not to give me grief, nor sorrow, nor pain, nor opposition. Please do not let anyone dislike me or betray me, and above all, do not ever let me feel forsaken by Thee or those I love. In fact, Lord, be careful to keep me from all the experiences that made Thee divine. And then, when the rough sledding by everyone else is over, please let me come and dwell with Thee, where I can boast about how similar our strengths and our characters are as I float along on my cloud of comfortable Christianity."[5]

The entire chapter of 2 Nephi 2 records Lehi's inspired teaching to his son about the need for opposing forces in God's plan of happiness. What is choosing righteousness without the real temptation to resist and rebel against God? Setbacks, mistakes, stumbling, falling, failures, or whatever you want to call them are part of God's plan of redemption for us in mortality. Through them all, we can learn to turn to the Lord, trust Him, and serve Him. God gave us "weakness that [we] may be humble" and if we will learn humility and faith before God, He has promised, "I will make weak things become strong unto [you]" (Ether 12:27).

In an address at a BYU Women's Conference, Francine R. Bennion described this truth using the three ways that Satan tempted Jesus at the beginning of His ministry as categories that equally apply to each of us:

> We wanted life, however high the cost. We suffer because we were willing to pay the cost of *being* and of being here with others in their ignorance and inexperience as well as our own. We suffer because we are willing to pay the costs of living with laws of nature, which operate quite consistently whether or not we understand them or can manage them. We suffer because, like Christ in the desert, we apparently did not say we would come only if God would change all our stones to

bread in time of hunger. We were willing to *know* hunger. Like Christ in the desert, we did not ask God to let us try falling or being bruised only on condition that he catch us before we touch ground and save us from real hurt. We were willing to *know* hurt. Like Christ, we did not agree to come only if God would make everyone bow to us and respect us, or admire us and understand us. Like Christ, we came to be ourselves, addressing and creating reality. We are finding out who we are and who we can become regardless of immediate environment or circumstances.[6]

Here's another truth to consider. Opposing forces don't always cancel each other. One side is not necessarily always good and the opposite side evil. Each side potentially holds value. I love the way Anne Morrow Lindbergh described how the ebb and flow of the tide can illustrate the value of intermittent, irregular, and opposing forces in relationships and, I would add, our progress along the covenant path. "We have so little faith in the ebb and flow of life, of love, of relationships. We leap at the flow of the tide and resist in terror its ebb. We are afraid it will never return. We insist on permanency, on duration, on continuity; when the only continuity possible, in life as in love, is in growth, in fluidity—in freedom. . . . Each cycle of the tide is valid; each cycle of the wave is valid; each cycle of a relationship is valid."[7] And, we could add, each cycle of life with its inherent opposition is valid. The ebb that opposes the flow can add color, texture, depth, wisdom, and appreciation that is not detectable in any other way. That is one reason why in our lowest, most tragic moments we can often feel God's warm embrace most poignantly. And why the Lord could reassure the Prophet Joseph in Liberty Jail, "All these things shall give thee experience, and shall be for thy good" (Doctrine and Covenants 122:7). Indeed, "it must needs be, that there is an opposition in all things," even when that opposition messes up some—or many—of our expectations (2 Nephi 2:11).

Although consequences of life in a fallen world interfere with our meticulous blueprint for an ideal life, unexpected benefits and compensatory blessings are available in opposition's wake. Elder Neal A. Maxwell shared how his disappointments and trials as a teenager allowed him to develop greater gifts. He explained, "In the spirit of candor and testimony, if that acne and those scars [from adolescence] added something to my capacity to have empathy, then it's worth it. If being left out socially, as I was at times, helps me to understand, it's worth it. If not achieving some temporal goal, like being all-state in basketball, helped me

OPPOSITION IN ALL THINGS

to understand what matters most, it's worth it. . . . It's because [the Lord] loves you that He is stretching your souls. . . . It's because He is a true father, who wants His children to be as happy as He is."[8]

People in multiple eras and at every age have discovered and celebrated the strengths that often come *only* through suffering and opposition. Here are a few of my favorite examples.

In the spring of 2024, speaking to the Stanford Graduate School of Business, the CEO for Nvidia (an American artificial intelligence company), Jensen Huang, connected suffering to expectations. He explained, "People with very high expectations have very low resilience—and unfortunately, resilience matters in success. . . . I don't know how to [teach resilience but] for all of you Stanford students, I wish upon you ample doses of pain and suffering. Greatness comes from character and character isn't formed out of smart people—it's formed out of people who suffered."[9] This was spoken by one of the most successful CEOs in the world, who immigrated to America at age nine, was bullied because of his race, and began his first paying job as a dishwasher at Denny's. He observed operations around him. He worked efficiently. And he applied what he learned, being promoted repeatedly, all while building resilience to forces that seemed to work against him. Great achievements came as results.

The essential presence of opposition was expounded in the seventeenth century. A renowned English author, John Milton, wrote an influential defense of freedom of the press in 1644 by drawing on the opposing conditions produced by the fall of Adam and Eve. To Milton, while the Fall at first appears to be a "doom" for humankind, it becomes the catalyst for learning to choose good because one sees the consequences of evil. Milton argued (original spelling retained),

> Good and evill we know in the field of this World grow up together almost inseparably; and the knowledge of good is so involv'd and interwoven with the knowledge of evill, and in so many cunning resemblances hardly to be discern'd.... And perhaps this is that doom which Adam fell into of knowing good and evill, that is to say of knowing good by evill. As therefore the state of man now is; what wisdome can there be to choose, what continence to forbeare without the knowledge of evill? He that can apprehend and consider vice with all her baits and seeming pleasures, and yet abstain, and

OPPOSITION IN ALL THINGS

yet distinguish, and yet prefer that which is truly better, he is the true wayfaring Christian.[10]

Milton recognized that it isn't in the absence of hardship, vice, and pain that we are transformed into holier, more Christlike beings. It is distinguishing and preferring good from evil when both are present, available, and enticing. Furthermore, being a true Christian is not in merely choosing good but *sincerely desiring* that which God loves when surrounded by influences that offend Him. A true Christian then willingly chooses to *act* upon those divine desires. Faith in Jesus Christ and our knowledge of truth require exercise to expand and grow strong. Such exercise is possible only when there is opposition in all things.

I even found this truth taught in a Hollywood movie. *Groundhog Day* humorously portrays the various possible outcomes if you could live the same day repeatedly. In it, a weatherman named Phil Connors (played by Bill Murray) considers himself "the talent" in every broadcast and believes that anyone is fortunate to be in his shadow. He is cocky, inconsiderate, and cynical. When he finds himself forced to relive the same day hundreds or possibly even thousands of times, he realizes that he is the only one who remembers what anyone said or did when the same day reopens on the morrow. In this cyclical and surreal world, Phil Connors experiments with manipulation, robbery, gluttony, a drunk-driving spree, and every other self-indulging behavior—because there are no consequences. Sensing no lasting joy or fulfillment from living his day that way, over time and through trial and error, Phil Connors begins using the day to develop new skills and experiments with compassionate responses to the people he repeatedly encounters. Along the way, Phil figures out what is most important in life. He becomes a new creature. Not just one who is playacting, but one who is new from the inside out. He chooses to change. He chooses to live each day with respect, compassion, and honor instead of with selfishness, lust, and greed. And he finally feels truly happy. In a related way, every new day gives us the invitation to learn from consequences from our actions the day before. We can choose to repent and change. In other words, we can repent every day and start anew. Repentance is not fantasy or fiction. Repentance is real and made possible *only* through our Redeemer and our choice to change. Like Phil, after thousands and thousands of days of repenting and trying to be more like Jesus, we too will become new creatures.

OPPOSITION IN ALL THINGS

Here is a final illustration. Back in the 1990s when Sister Janette Hales was named Young Women General President, she shared with her general board how overwhelming it felt to be responsible for so many thousands of precious young women all over the world. In a whimsical moment and with her deadpan humor, she asked, "Wouldn't it be great if we could just lock them all up in the temple until they turned twenty?" We all laughed at her fanciful musings.

Later, I was speaking to a small group of young men and young women. I told them what President Hales had facetiously imagined about locking up all the youth in the temple to keep them safe from temptation until they were out of their teens. Then I asked: "Even if we COULD do that, what would make it wrong? Why would locking you up in the temple be an unwise solution for protecting you youth?" No one answered for several seconds. Then from the front row, one of the newest-minted Beehives (the former name of the class for twelve- to thirteen-year-old girls in the Church) raised her hand. She simply stated, "You'd learn to hate the temple." I've never forgotten her answer. Satan wanted to do something similar. He would ensure no one ever made a bad decision or suffered pain in mortality. Basically, Satan wanted to give us no option but to "live in the temple" continually. We could never choose good or evil, let alone *become* righteous, if righteousness were the only choice.

The purpose of this life is not simply to give the appearance of being good, but to *become* a better person through our choices and the process of repentance. Elder Dale G. Renlund astutely distinguished the difference this way: "Our Heavenly Father's goal in parenting is not to have His children *do* what is right; it is to have His children *choose* to do what is right and ultimately become like Him.... God is not interested in His children just becoming trained and obedient 'pets' who will not chew on His slippers in the celestial living room. No, God wants His children to grow up spiritually and join Him in the family business."[11]

Similarly, President Thomas S. Monson recognized the temptation to see Heavenly Father's promise to the faithful as removal of trials and loss before they happen. He cautioned,

> Some of you may at times have cried out in your suffering, wondering why our Heavenly

OPPOSITION IN ALL THINGS

Father would allow you to go through whatever trials you are facing. . . .

Our mortal life, however, was never meant to be easy or consistently pleasant. Our Heavenly Father . . . knows that we learn and grow and become refined through hard challenges, heartbreaking sorrows, and difficult choices. Each one of us experiences dark days when our loved ones pass away, painful times when our health is lost, feelings of being forsaken when those we love seem to have abandoned us. These and other trials present us with the real test of our ability to endure.[12]

As daughters and sons of Eve and Adam, we inherit the consequences of this fallen world, including opposition in all things. And because we can learn so much from the process, our expectations can be refined and better informed by our experiences.

CHAPTER FOUR

Our Bodies Are Mortal

4

The restored gospel teaches that God created this world to be governed by natural law and personal agency. Elder Taylor G. Godoy reminded us, "This life, by its nature, brings painful experiences, some inherent to our physical bodies, some due to our weaknesses or afflictions, some due to the way others use their agency, and some due to our use of agency."[1] This chapter discusses how life in a world governed by natural law often upsets our plans for the future, especially when our mortal bodies seem to suddenly fail us.

Opposing forces appear everywhere in nature and in response to natural law. Gravity, entropy, aging, germs, allergies, viruses, bacteria, genetics, temperature extremes, atmospheric pressure, ferocious weather, fire, and water can dramatically alter our expectations and options.

Consequences from any of these forces can be unfair, precarious, and life-altering.

One of the biggest influences on unmet expectations is unanticipated changes in our mortal bodies. Fatal diseases, debilitating accidents, and attacks on our muscles, nerves, and brain can diminish our physical and mental abilities—and therefore, our options—sooner than we imagine. A quick survey of any subgroup in the Church will indicate there is no magic formula for guaranteeing a long life of continual good health and activity. As my grandfather used to quote from his souvenir wall plaque: "We be too soon old and too late smart!" Some people defy the odds for a long time, but eventually, we all become intimately acquainted with sagging muscles, waning energy, sluggish minds, and a slower pace. Our physical bodies are not immune to the laws of entropy and gravity. Learning to progress amid natural law is all part of the plan to teach us what God offers in this fallen world.

> Learning to progress amid natural law is all part of the plan.

When we are young, we can't imagine how our mortal bodies could ever betray us. We get up and run when we want, thrive on little sleep, and eat without fear for our health. We see elderly people shuffle along and their mental acuity diminish while we think we will remain young

OUR BODIES ARE MORTAL

forever. We may be very health conscious in our choice of foods and pay attention to regular exercise. We may think that if we remain active and engaged, committed to a healthy diet, we can ward off the diseases and symptoms that affect so many around us. Even if we haven't had the healthiest of lifestyles, we strive to at least live the Word of Wisdom. That promises to protect our bodies from poor performance, disease, and slowing down. Doesn't it? *But if not . . .*

President Dieter F. Uchtdorf discovered an answer to this conundrum, but not until much later in his life.

> I remember when I was preparing to be trained as a fighter pilot. We spent a great deal of our preliminary military training in physical exercise. . . .
>
> As I was running I began to notice something that, frankly, troubled me. Time and again I was being passed by men who smoked, drank, and did all manner of things that were contrary to the gospel and, in particular, to the Word of Wisdom.
>
> I remember thinking, "Wait a minute! Aren't I supposed to be able to run and not be weary?" But I *was* weary, and I was overtaken by people who were definitely not following the Word of Wisdom.

I confess, it troubled me at the time. I asked myself, was the promise true or was it not?

The answer didn't come immediately. But eventually I learned that God's promises are not always fulfilled as quickly as or in the way we might hope; they come according to His timing and in His ways. Years later I could see clear evidence of the temporal blessings that come to those who obey the Word of Wisdom—in addition to the spiritual blessings that come immediately from obedience to any of God's laws. Looking back, I know for sure that the promises of the Lord, if perhaps not always swift, are always certain.[2]

President Boyd K. Packer wisely observed, "The Word of Wisdom does not promise you perfect health, but it teaches how to keep the body you were born with in the best condition and your mind alert to delicate spiritual promptings."[3] While susceptible to the laws of nature, our mortal bodies receive a measure of protection from adhering to the Word of Wisdom that we would not have obtained otherwise.

Furthermore, celestial glory is not granted by maintaining robust health in mortality. Although President Russell M. Nelson has enjoyed great health and activity—for one hundred years!—he recognizes that perfect bodies are not requisite to fulfilling God's plan for us. He cautioned:

> Please note: A perfect body is not required to achieve a divine destiny. In fact, some of the sweetest spirits are housed in frail frames. Great spiritual strength is often developed by those with physical challenges—precisely because they are challenged. Such individuals are entitled to all the blessings that God has in store for His faithful and obedient children. . . .
>
> When we truly know our divine nature, . . . we will focus our eyes on sights, our ears on sounds, and our minds on thoughts that are a credit to our physical creation as a temple of God. In daily prayer, we will gratefully acknowledge Him as our Creator and thank Him for the magnificence of our own physical temple. We will care for it and cherish it as our own personal gift from God.[4]

Sometimes the state of our bodies' health tutors us in our desires to become more like the Savior in ways we couldn't learn any other way. Again, suffering is part of the plan and has the potential to be remarkably instructive. Instead of asking *why* this happened to us or our loved one, we might ask who has been with us throughout the ordeal.

> Instead of asking *why* this happened to us or our loved one, we might ask who has been with us throughout the ordeal.

In such tender times, feeling the presence of God or His angels is not uncommon. We are not alone.

The best way I know to teach this is by hearing testimonials of those who have experienced it.

Patricia Parkinson was born with good eyesight but began losing it at age seven and was blind at age eleven. When her young nephew asked her why she hadn't asked Heavenly Father for new eyes because He gives us whatever we want, Pat answered, "Well, sometimes Heavenly Father doesn't work like that. Sometimes He needs you to learn something, and so He doesn't give you everything you want. Sometimes you have to wait. Heavenly Father and the Savior know best what is good for us and what we need. So They aren't going to grant you everything you want in the moment you want it."

Because Elder Brook P. Hales of the Seventy had known Pat for many years, he had opportunities to see how she responded to her unexpected life with a disability. He expressed his admiration for her positive and happy attitude, to which Pat replied, "Well, you have not been at home with me, have you? I have my moments. I've had rather severe bouts of depression, and I've cried a lot. . . .

OUR BODIES ARE MORTAL

From the time I started losing my sight, it was strange, but I knew that Heavenly Father and the Savior were with my family and me. . . . I have ended up being a successful enough person, and generally I have been a happy person. . . . To those who ask me if I am angry because I am blind, I respond, 'Who would I be angry with? Heavenly Father is in this with me; I am not alone. He is with me all the time.'"[5]

Pat did not imply that her life was ideal; she learned to accept that mortality includes the likelihood of loss of physical abilities. Rather than dwelling on her losses, however, Pat used her disability to find God in her life. Her loss of physical eyesight led her to see God's presence more clearly.

A religion scholar, Kate Bowler, was living her dream as the wife of an ideal man, the mother of a miracle son, and in her dream job as a professor at Duke Divinity School. She had already received prominence for her research and writing on the prosperity gospel (introduced briefly in chapter 2). Though not initially a believer in the prosperity gospel, she started to believe it when others in the movement touted her as a poster child due to her incredibly good fortune in health, wealth, and academic notoriety. And then at age thirty-five, she was diagnosed with stage IV colon cancer. Out of nowhere.

BUT IF NOT

In a touching, humorous, and heart-wrenching memoir of her continuing struggle for survival after the diagnosis, she shares insight into more meaningful living while learning about dying. She concludes that her illness did not come as a punishment for displeasing God or because she didn't do enough good. She doesn't ask that question. Instead, she reads letters from fellow sufferers who speak of Someone who was with them when they thought the end had come. One man wrote her that he "doesn't rationalize why some people are rescued and others are not. . . . But he knows that God was there [in his time of terror] because he felt peace, indescribable peace, and it changed him forever."[6]

Kate learned to avoid the trap that claims that God punishes us when we displease Him, even when believers around her told her otherwise. Instead of asking "why me?" she sought understanding from fellow sufferers who had discovered peace and hope. Empathy for someone suffering serious illness is a blessing that can be learned through similar suffering.

Elder Neal A. Maxwell recognized a deeper way to teach the gospel of Jesus Christ because he endured years of serious illness. Shortly before being diagnosed with leukemia, he wrote an article entitled "Enduring Well," in which he observed, "Certain forms of suffering, endured well, can actually be ennobling. . . . Part of enduring well consists of being meek enough, amid our suffering, to learn from our relevant experiences . . . in ways which sanctify us." After enduring the effects of cancer and its treatment for three years, while "in a pondering mood about his illness, . . . the soul voice of the Spirit came into his mind to whisper, 'I have given you leukemia that you might teach my people with authenticity.'"[7] This personal revelation to one of the Twelve is not to suggest that God is responsible for giving diseases and serious illness to everyone. In this specific instance, Elder Maxwell learned that suffering from cancer was part of his mortal education to complete his personal mission as God deemed important. During those three years, Elder Maxwell learned a deeper understanding of what it means to endure well than even he, with his profound insight, had previously known.

Finally, physical pain and death can open our eyes to less obvious miracles that God performs in our lives. As a young man, Elder Brent H. Nielson had just returned from his mission when his father was diagnosed with pancreatic cancer. His father and his entire family had great faith that he would be healed and soon return to normal life activities. Rather than a miraculous healing occurring, his father's cancer spread rapidly and took his life in a matter of months. After the funeral, Elder Nielson said, "I began to wonder why my father had not been healed. I wondered if my faith was not strong enough. Why did some families receive a miracle, but our family did not?" Through searching and pondering scriptural accounts of the Savior's healing miracles, Elder Nielson concluded,

> I had mistakenly believed that the Savior's healing power had not worked for my family. As I now look back with more mature eyes and experience, I see that the Savior's healing power was evident in the lives of each of my family members. I was so focused on a physical healing that I failed to see the miracles that had occurred. The Lord strengthened and lifted my mother beyond her capacity through this difficult trial, and she led a long and productive life. She had a remarkable positive influence on her children and grandchildren. The Lord blessed me and my siblings with love, unity, faith, and resilience that became an important part of our lives and continues today.[8]

Premature deaths, loss of physical ability, mental deterioration, and the natural aging process nearly always upset our expectations for the future. In His own way, however, God seems poised to grant individually designed blessings that open new doors of learning, understanding, and becoming that always lead us into a closer relationship with Him. A quote frequently attributed to Elder Orson F. Whitney (a member of the Quorum of the Twelve from 1906 to 1931) teaches,

> No pain that we suffer, no trial that we experience is wasted. It ministers to our education, to the development of such qualities as patience, faith, fortitude and humility. All that we suffer and all that we endure, especially when we endure it patiently, builds up our characters, purifies our hearts, expands our souls, and makes us more tender and charitable, more worthy to be called the children of God . . . and it is through sorrow and suffering, toil and tribulation, that we gain the education that we come here to acquire and which will make us more like our Father and Mother in heaven.[9]

Does our loyalty to the Lord depend on our continued good health? *But if not.* Our lives may not be what we dreamed of, especially when our bodies lose their vitality and acuity, but we can't help but feel gratitude and love for the One who knows more than we do. We are not alone. He is watching over us and giving us hope to still dream.

CHAPTER FIVE

Agency vs. Expectations

5

Agency (our own and that of others) is dynamic and fluid. Doors of opportunity open and close constantly because we are each free to choose. This reality produces any number of possible outcomes, some favorable and others not at all. For example, even having complete control of our own agency, we can sabotage our future opportunities and introduce more suffering, needless suffering, than what naturally occurs in a fallen world. When others choose to reject God's laws of love and kindness, actions we cannot control can jeopardize our own personal plans. Additionally, those we love may choose a path that conflicts with our values, causing us to question what we did wrong. These dynamic conditions and many others dismantle our expectations, requiring us to readjust and redirect. In a fallen world, anything can happen when opposing agencies collide.

BUT IF NOT

Take for instance, when our own choices jeopardize future options. Decisions we make can eliminate certain opportunities, create unwanted detours, and disrupt our life dreams. The prodigal son is a case in point (see Luke 15:11–32). In the parable, he alone chose to take his inheritance and leave home. He alone decided to "waste" that inheritance on riotous living. In the end, he chose to repent and return home only to discover his father's merciful and generous blessing. But what future opportunities did he lose because he "wasted" so many years in selfish, decadent living?

President Henry B. Eyring shared a personal experience that taught him this truth of lost opportunities. He told of a man who had been ordained a deacon at age twelve but soon afterwards chose the excitement of the world rather than obedience to God. When he finally came to himself, he had lost his wife, his children, an eye, and every material thing that he owned except that which fit into a little trunk. A copy of the Book of Mormon had long before been buried in that trunk and, along with it, an invitation to return to the Lord. When the man eventually found the book, he accepted that invitation, and in his seventies was a district missionary serving with a young companion named Henry B. Eyring. During a missionary lesson with a family living in a trailer, then-Elder Eyring

AGENCY VS. EXPECTATIONS

used his repentant companion as an example of complete forgiveness:

> I asked the people we were teaching, as I testified of the power of the Savior's Atonement, to look at [my companion]. He had been washed clean and given a new heart, and I knew they would see that in his face. I told the people that what they saw was evidence that the Atonement of Jesus Christ could wash away *all* the corrosive effects of sin.
>
> That was the only time [my companion] ever rebuked me. He told me in the darkness outside the trailer where we had been teaching that I should have told the people that while God was able to give him a new heart, He had not been able to give him back his wife and his children and what he might have done for them. . . . He moved forward, lifted by faith, to what yet might be.[1]

Like the prodigal son, this man was completely forgiven by the Father and had every hope for eternal life, but his chance to enjoy the blessings of the gospel in mortality with his wife and children had vanished.

We may suffer unnecessarily in another way. By misunderstanding the doctrine of opposition in all things, we may take the pain and suffering that others inflict upon us as a badge of honor. Yes, we will all experience pain and sorrow in mortality, but that does not necessitate that we submit to those who use their agency for evil against us. We are all too aware of such tragic cases. An abused wife remains a victim in a marriage because she incorrectly assumes that her marriage covenant requires her to endure whatever her husband inflicts. No divine law tolerates verbal, physical, or sexual abuse. Period. We live at a time when hatred and revenge are loudly expressed all around us. Racism, sexism, war, and hostility against certain religions have escalated. Domestic violence, bullying, and road rage are all too common. Some people are inflicting horrible, unthinkable suffering on others without any sense of remorse. God does not require us to suffer in this way. For those of us fortunate to be safe from abusive environments, we can choose to do much to free and protect those who are being harmed.

I have explored how decisions over which we have at least some control can disrupt our life's plans. In a very different way, another person's use of their agency can upend our plans and dreams every bit as much. What happens when someone makes decisions that interfere with our personal life? When individuals choose to act with greed, unrighteous dominion, pride, stupidity, etc., oftentimes

AGENCY VS. EXPECTATIONS

those with no choice in the matter are affected adversely and even seriously harmed. If you are one who has been the victim of such unfairness, you know how excruciatingly painful it can be.

Sometimes the wrongdoer in such cases even appears to flourish. For instance, a well-qualified candidate may be eliminated from potential hire because of personal jealousy while an unqualified friend of the company is hired and given a lucrative career. A confused and angry youth may choose to drive drunk and subsequently crash into a young family returning home. The accident may then lead the driver to finally get the help he needs to stay sober. An attorney may care only about her record for winning, and so builds a case that falsely accuses an innocent defendant that harms the defendant's reputation and future opportunities. Mistakes and sins of others often cause great suffering to the innocent and undeserved perks for the guilty.

Other times, the victim of another's unrighteous actions may even end up in a better situation after being harmed or taken advantage of. In such cases, we may then be tempted to think that God inspired the evil person to direct the innocent one toward success, even if it was done in spite. Importantly, God does not inspire anyone to harm or denigrate another person. For any reason. For instance, I could maliciously cause you loss, suffering, or logistical nightmares that inadvertently set you on a path to success. To later justify my cruelty toward you, I may claim that God must have not wanted you to be offered that job that I kept you from, or to marry that person, or to win that legal conflict, or to move to that part of the world, so He inspired *me* to block your way. Just because God prepares a new path for you, however, does not justify my cruelty and lack of integrity.

President Joseph Fielding Smith taught that God never foreordained anyone to sin, just as He doesn't constrain any to do good. He honors our agency, whether we choose to use it for good or for evil. President Smith testified,

> No person was foreordained or appointed to sin or to perform a mission of evil. No person is ever predestined to salvation or damnation. Every person has free agency. Cain was promised by the Lord that if he would do well, he would be accepted. Judas had his agency and acted upon it; no [divine] pressure was brought to bear on him to cause him to betray the Lord, but he was led by Lucifer. If men were appointed to sin and betray their brethren, then justice could not demand that they be punished for sin and betrayal when they are guilty.[2]

AGENCY VS. EXPECTATIONS

To one day become like our Father, we also need to learn to recognize another's agency. One of the most heart-wrenching circumstances dealing with personal agency is when someone close to us chooses a path other than what we feel is best for them. Perhaps one of the hardest to navigate is when a loved one chooses to leave the Church we love. Many of our heroes in scripture have grappled with heartache and disappointment when a child chooses a different path. Lehi and Sariah continued to love and include Laman and Lemuel even when they rebelled against God's commands. Alma the Elder pleaded with God for help with his wayward son Alma, as did King Mosiah, whose four sons used their agency to join with Alma the Younger and fight against the Church.

Certainly, God understands such pain and weeps over His children who choose to reject the warmth of His covenantal embrace. When Enoch asked how "the God of heaven" could weep when His children rebelled against His commandments, the Lord answered, "Behold these . . . are the workmanship of mine own hands . . . and in the Garden of Eden, gave I unto man his agency; and unto thy brethren have I . . . given commandment, that they should love one another, and that they should choose me, their Father; but behold, they are without affection, and they hate their own blood" (Moses 7:28, 32–33). To sincerely love another is to be vulnerable to heartbreak, as our Father certainly knows all too well.

God also knows the value of time and experiencing the consequences of our choices in the learning process of becoming like Him. And He is patient. Very patient. Can we trust God's timetable and ability to rescue our loved ones? While giving those we love space to learn God's will for them, we can create an environment of love where they can be reminded of the Savior's constant awareness, healing balm, and enabling power.

> Can we trust God's timetable and ability to rescue our loved ones?

Frederik Hegner Odgaard experienced a broken heart after returning from his mission to find that his beloved nineteen-year-old brother no longer wanted to participate in the Church. Frederik's mission had taught him to ask inspired questions and to listen to answers with compassion and patience. So, he spent time showing his brother that he would love and care for him even when his brother didn't choose the gospel. After two years, he reported that his relationship with his brother was still good. "We don't talk about the gospel much, but we talk about other things. I still wish that we could have the gospel in common, but we do have a lot of other things in common. We still hang out and do things together, and I love him for who he is."

AGENCY VS. EXPECTATIONS

Frederik concluded, "We can't always control the actions of others, especially when it comes to matters of strengthening our faith or living the gospel. But I know that even if those we love most in the world have challenges of faith, when we prioritize God and follow His will and strive to hear Him, we will always be blessed with answers, with a strong testimony, and with the spiritual revelation we need to keep following Him."[3]

God hasn't given up on Frederik's brother and neither has Frederik. Taking the long view, our trust in the Lord's healing power can be strengthened as we show our love for those who no longer believe by rejoicing in all that is still so very, very good in them.

Miracles happen every day in the world. Lost souls sincerely repent, hearts change, sealed doors suddenly open, and wounds heal. We long for such miracles for those we love. And we long for them today. *But if not.* Answers from scripture and latter-day prophets suggest there is no formulaic reason that satisfies every circumstance when personal agencies collide. Sometimes God does indeed intercede, and other times it feels like no Divine Hand

> Our trust in the Lord's healing power can be strengthened as we show our love for those who no longer believe by rejoicing in all that is still so very, very good in them.

is reaching out to help. These are among the conundrums we continually navigate in mortality. Always, however, God offers confirmation that He is aware of us and that He provides compensatory blessings.[4] While talk of compensatory blessings at the time of our deepest loss is like ripping open our wounds, given time—most often LOTS of time, with the balm of the Atoning One, those wounds will heal. In every way, Jesus Christ came to "bind up the brokenhearted" (Isaiah 61:1). And He arises "with healing in his wings" (Malachi 4:2).

Consider a few examples of how sometimes the innocent and righteous are shielded from the consequences of others' choices, while at other times, they suffer deep pain and loss. In such examples, look for the Lord's compensatory gifts to the believers.

Alma and Almulek warned the wicked Ammonihahites that "their torments [of spiritual death] shall be as a lake of fire and brimstone" (Alma 12:17). In response, the Ammonihahites cast out of their city all of the believing men. But that was not all. They next threw into their own "lake of fire and brimstone" all the believing women and children of the city. Their wickedness included inflicting psychological trauma on the survivors, including the missionary witnesses.[5] Amulek asked Alma if they couldn't

AGENCY VS. EXPECTATIONS

"exercise the power of God which is in us, and save them from the flames" (Alma 14:10).

We can relate to Amulek's desire to use priesthood power to save the innocent from pain and death. After all, the Lord demonstrated His power in dramatically preserving Meshach, Shadrach, and Abed-nego from fiery flames, right? *But if not* . . . Alma's response to Amulek's request underscores that God honors agency, and in this case did not intercede to save innocent lives or protect the missionaries from witnessing the tragedy. Alma told Amulek, "The Spirit constraineth me that I must not stretch forth mine hand; for behold the Lord receiveth them [the believing women and children] up unto himself, in glory; and he doth suffer that . . . the people may do this thing unto them, according to the hardness of their hearts, that the judgments which he shall exercise upon them in his wrath may be just; and the blood of the innocent shall stand as a witness against them, yea, and cry mightily against them at the last day" (Alma 14:11).

Knowledge of the Lord's awareness and acceptance of these precious souls did not return them to their husbands and fathers, but it had the potential to comfort those left behind in their deep loss. Elder James E. Talmage wrote, "No pang that is suffered by man or woman on the earth will be without its compensating effect . . . if it be met with patience."⁶ Again, "let patience have her perfect work" to give space for our trust in the Lord to deepen and our conviction of His grace to expand (James 1:4).

Father Lehi recognized that his young son Jacob had "suffered afflictions and much sorrow, because of the rudeness of thy brethren," but assured him that "God . . . shall consecrate thine afflictions for thy gain" (2 Nephi 2:1–2; see also 32:9). We get a sense of the Lord's blessings and strong presence in Jacob's later life from his inspired writings in the Book of Mormon. But what about his rude brothers? Is their cruelty to their little brother so quickly erased?

Interestingly, Lehi didn't specify which of the brothers caused young Jacob affliction. We can easily assume it was the perpetual "baddies," Laman and Lemuel, but that isn't what Lehi said. Did it include Jacob's "good" brothers, too? It is difficult to find any weakness in Nephi's record, but he admitted at times that he needed to have his heart softened and his "iniquities" forgiven (see 1 Nephi 2:16; 2 Nephi 4:17–18, 27). The imprecise verbiage of "brothers" at least opens our minds to the possibility that well-meaning individuals may harm others at times.⁷ The fact that God sent Jacob compensatory blessings didn't excuse his brothers' unkind treatment. The Lord is aware of the harm bullies inflict. So, we are left to trust in His wisdom in showing

AGENCY VS. EXPECTATIONS

mercy and grace in ways that will best shape His children into glorious vessels.

In reviewing a long list of men and women who were so sure of God's promises that they acted in faith even when there was no physical evidence to validate them, the author of Hebrews observed that "these all died in faith, not having received the promises, but having seen them afar off, and were persuaded of them, and embraced them" (Hebrews 11:13). These individuals' faith in God was unshakable. They were so sure of what God promised that they acted as though those promises were already fulfilled (see Joseph Smith Translation, Hebrews 11:1). *But if not?* Many of them died before they saw the promised outcomes. Talk about unmet expectations! The eleventh chapter of Hebrews bears witness that whether the promises are fulfilled in this life or the next, those with unwavering faith die with the assurance that God always keeps His promises.

The same chapter hints at the seeming randomness of suffering and rescue: "Women received their dead raised to life again: and others were tortured, not accepting deliverance; that they might obtain a better resurrection" (Hebrews 11:35). Some children are miraculously saved while other children suffer for no lawful reason. These mothers continued in faith notwithstanding.

The scriptures contain numerous other examples of when God intervened and when He did not. King Noah and his wicked priests burned the great prophet Abinadi at the stake because of his testimony of Jesus Christ while Alma, one of those wicked priests, was miraculously preserved after he believed in Abinadi's words (see Mosiah 17). The life of every single one of the stripling warriors was saved because of their great faith in the Lord (see Alma 56). On the other hand, at least some of those young men must have suffered the loss of their fathers who honored covenants with God and buried their weapons of war rather than shed any more blood (see Alma 24). In New Testament Israel, King Herod imprisoned Peter and James for their preaching of Christ while all the believers met together to pray *for both*; however, James was killed by the sword in prison and Peter was miraculously freed by an angel (see Acts 12). And Abraham was saved from death by an angel on the same altar where the three daughters of Onitah had been slain because they would not deny their testimonies of God (see Abraham 1:8–18). This apparent randomness occurs in all eras among all peoples and cannot be explained by saying the blessed ones were righteous and those who suffered must have offended God. *But if not.* In this fallen world, bad things happen to good people all the time in part because we live among fellow humans

AGENCY VS. EXPECTATIONS

who make evil choices and their victims suffer the consequences.

I have found President Dallin H. Oaks's reminder helpful in this regard: "God rarely infringes on the agency of any of His children by intervening against some for the relief of others. But He does ease the burdens of our afflictions and strengthen us to bear them, as He did for Alma's people in the land of Helam (see Mosiah 24:13–15). He does not prevent all disasters, but He does answer our prayers to turn them aside, . . . or [to] blunt their effects."[8]

In an emotional address to the Church after miraculously recovering from a life-threatening illness while suffering the recent loss of his beloved wife Pat, President Jeffrey R. Holland reflected on his personal wrestle with opposing answers to prayer. He remarked, "I recognize that at roughly the same time so many were praying for the restoration of my health, an equal number—including me—were praying for the restoration of my wife's health. I testify that both of those prayers were heard *and* answered by a divinely compassionate Heavenly Father, even if the prayers for Pat were *not* answered the way I asked."[9] God gave us prayer not to direct and educate *Him* on our personal needs and desires, but to educate and refine *our desires* to grow in faith.

direct and educate *Him* on our personal needs and desires, but to educate and refine *our desires* to grow in faith. We then can acknowledge that He sees and knows more than we do. A lot more.

In God's omniscience, He provided us a mortal environment where we may choose to follow the covenant path and turn away from the hateful and violent despite the immediate outcome. Along that sometimes treacherous and painful path, we will discover that our questions become more intense, profound, and meaningful. Personal revelation increases and expands as it grows out of deep, intense anguish. In the words of one of our hymns:

> *Does the journey seem long,*
> *The path rugged and steep?*
> *Are there briars and thorns on the way?*
> *Do sharp stones cut your feet*
> *As you struggle to rise*
> *To the heights thru the heat of the day?*
>
> *Let your heart be not faint*
> *Now the journey's begun;*
> *There is One who still beckons to you.*
> *So look upward in joy*
> *And take hold of his hand;*
> *He will lead you to heights that are new.*[10]

AGENCY VS. EXPECTATIONS

When we view this mortal journey through an eye of faith, the loss of some of our expectations isn't such an exorbitant price to pay for greater direction, revelation, and wisdom. Having Him with us to teach, direct, and transform us to become more like Him is always miraculous.

CHAPTER SIX

Divinely Designed Paths

6

God knows us better than we do and sees much farther into the future than we can. With His long view of our mortality, He may invite us to take a lesser-known trail along the covenant path that we cannot see. Elder D. Todd Christofferson taught, "Our Father is willing to guide each of us along His covenant path with steps designed to our individual need and tailored to his plan for our ultimate happiness with Him."[1] Another reason our expectations don't materialize is because God has something better in mind for us. In truth, even when we have been beaten up by the storms of life and seemingly doomed to failure, the Lord in His wisdom and power brings beauty from ashes (see Isaiah 61:3). We still have reason to hope and to dream. God's path for us may feel like an overgrown maze of dead ends and roads to nowhere until later in life when, looking back, we begin to recognize beautiful patterns with a clear

BUT IF NOT

purpose that were indiscernible when experienced in the moment.

One of the great blessings of getting older is that you have the benefit of hindsight. When we are young, it is easy to get frustrated because you can't imagine how a current "setback" or "failure" could lead anywhere productive. Over time, however, you look back and with wonder detect a clear path that led to opened doors of opportunity you never knew existed and avenues for growth and contribution you now cherish. The Lord gave us a way to test this claim. He stated, "As often as thou hast inquired thou hast received instruction of my Spirit. If it had not been so, thou wouldst not have come to the place where thou art at this time" (Doctrine and Covenants 6:14). I have personally received answers to prayer by applying the Lord's hindsight test. I can testify that it works.

Similarly, President Dieter F. Uchtdorf observed, "Often the deep valleys of our present will be understood only by looking back on them from the mountains of our future experience. Often we can't see the Lord's hand in our lives until long after trials have passed. Often the most difficult times of our lives are essential building blocks that form the foundation of our character and pave the way to future opportunity, understanding, and happiness."[2]

Without the benefit of hindsight, *during* those times of

DIVINELY DESIGNED PATHS

uncertainty, when we cannot imagine how our lives can ever get back on track, thinking of turning our lives over to God often seems impossible. Then serving as Primary General President, Camille N. Johnson asked why we often put off asking God what He wants us to do to progress when we know He is all-loving and truthful. She suggested,

> Perhaps it is because we don't have the faith to accept the answer we might receive. Perhaps it is because the natural man or woman in us is resistant to turning things *completely* over to the Lord and trusting Him *entirely*. Maybe that is why we choose to stick with the narrative we have written for ourselves, a comfortable version of our story unedited by the Master Author. We don't want to ask a question and get an answer that doesn't fit neatly into the story we are writing for ourselves.[3]

I can relate to what President Johnson taught. In a similar vein, I have often said, if we let Him, God will take us to that place where only He can help us. It is in that place where we begin to glimpse that with God, we can assuredly do ALL things He desires for us. Because He honors our agency, we can choose not to let Him direct our paths. We can choose to never leave our comfort zone. We may choose a path with no steep incline at all. And we can

BUT IF NOT

subsequently never learn what we are capable of. Or we can let Him lead us. We will *always* accomplish more if we turn our lives over to God rather than act on our fears or insist that we know better than He does.

President Hugh B. Brown, a former member of the First Presidency, presented one of the most endearing talks on letting God prevail in our lives when the future appears doomed. His remarks remain deeply relevant over fifty years later.[4] Speaking at Brigham Young University commencement exercises, President Brown assured the graduates,

> Now some of you as you go forward are going to meet with disappointment—perhaps many disappointments, some of them crucial. Sometimes you will wonder if God has forgotten you. Sometimes you may even wonder if He lives and where He has gone. But in these times [of uncertainty], . . . I think I could not leave . . . a better message than this: God is aware of you individually. He knows who you are and what you are, and, furthermore, He knows what you are capable of becoming. Be not discouraged, then, if you do not get all the things you want just when you want them. Have the courage to go on and face your

DIVINELY DESIGNED PATHS

life and, if necessary, reverse it to bring it into harmony with His law.

President Brown continued by recounting a personal experience when, as a young man, he cut back a large, overgrown currant bush. In an imaginary conversation with the now-dramatically pruned plant, the currant bush seemed to ask the gardener why he would cut him back after he had worked so hard to grow tall. To which the gardener responded, "Look, little currant bush, I *am* the gardener here, and I know what I want you to be. If I let you go the way you want to go, you will never amount to anything. But someday, when you are laden with fruit, you are going to think back and say, 'Thank you, Mr. Gardener, for cutting me down, for loving me enough to hurt me.'"

President Brown linked this experience to one he had just ten years later when, during World War I, he was next in line to be appointed a general in the Canadian army, a position he "had cherished in [his] heart for years." Reporting to his commanding officer, young Officer Brown was full of confidence that he would walk back out with the new commission. In less than a minute, however, his commanding officer dashed all his expectations with one brief announcement: "Brown, you are entitled to this promotion, but I cannot make it. You have qualified and passed the regulations, you have had the experience, and you are entitled to it in every way, but I cannot make this appointment." When Officer Brown glanced down at his personal history sheet on the general's desk, he saw large words printed in capital letters: "THIS MAN IS A MORMON."

Feeling like a failure for not receiving the promotion and filled with bitterness and anger, Officer Brown returned to his tent and shook his fist toward heaven, shouting, "How could you do this to me, God? I've done everything that I knew how to do to uphold the standards of the Church. I was making such wonderful growth, and now you've cut me down. How could you do it?" That is when he seemed to hear a voice respond, "I am the gardener here. I know what I want you to be. If I let you go the way you want to go, you will never amount to anything. And someday, when you are ripened in life, you are going to shout back across the time and say, 'Thank you, Mr. Gardener, for cutting me down, for loving me enough to hurt me.'" Recognizing his words to the currant bush a decade before, Officer Brown was immediately humbled and "prayed for forgiveness for my arrogance and my ambition."[5]

Hugh B. Brown clearly deserved and had already earned that promotion. *But if not.* The Lord had other plans for him. When the Lord cuts us back, it isn't abusive

DIVINELY DESIGNED PATHS

in the belittling and harmful ways we hear of today. His chastening is always for our good. Remember that the root word for chasten is *chaste*. God's pruning leads us to be purer, nobler, and better than we were before. After the war, President Brown served the Lord in meaningful ways before being called to the Quorum of the Twelve and then to the First Presidency. His example of courage and faith in living and teaching the gospel of Jesus Christ has inspired and guided countless individuals who never met him, including me. I can't imagine how his influence could have been greater should he have instead attained his dream of impressive military rank.

As remarkable as President Brown's story is, we may conclude that of course, God has individualized assignments in mind for the senior leaders of His Church, but why would He have a personalized path for those of us in the rank and file? I believe He does. Each one of us is evidence of His individualized tutelage and personalized plan—as well as our choice to follow it or not.

If you and I were visiting together on your front porch, this is where I would ask you to relate your story. When you look back on your life, where do you see a Divine Hand leading you through a door you hadn't noticed? Did you accept His invitation? Where did it lead? How is your life's story different as a result?

Because you were brave enough to share your story with me, I would then share my story with you. I am often asked how a girl from small-town northern Utah ended up being a professor of ancient scripture at BYU. It's a long story. I won't go through all the details, but it wasn't what I expected. Not even close. Nor was it applauded by most people who knew me. When I was considering serving a mission for the Church at age twenty-one (because I wanted to better understand the doctrine of the Church and share it with others), I was told that because I was a girl, I didn't need to learn more than I already knew. Along the way, many observers expressed chagrin over my future: You need to learn how to flirt. Stop being so picky. No one wants to marry a girl with a lot of education. You already have two strikes against you—an undergraduate degree and a full-time mission. A graduate degree would be strike three. What can you do with such an obscure graduate degree?

I always dreamed and planned to marry and have a family. But that isn't a goal you achieve on your own. To be honest, guys were not knocking on my door interested in getting to know me. And while my undergraduate degree

> When you look back on your life, where do you see a Divine Hand leading you through a door you hadn't noticed? Did you accept His invitation? Where did it lead?

and mission closed a lot of dating doors, my academic achievements swung open completely different doors. And just the opposite from my experiences with eligible young men, I was actively pursued for employment without even applying. It all started when I was offered a full-time job teaching seminary for the Church. There were no women teaching full-time seminary for the Church at the time. None. Zero. That, however, didn't seem to matter. The teaching-seminary-door stood wide open to me while all the traditional doors were soundly shut. So, I accepted the offer.

Being the only woman in the Church being paid a salary to teach seminary at the time turned a lot of heads, but not the heads of potential marriage partners. Some said my life was the LDS equivalent of being a Catholic nun. On the other hand, doors to teaching, advanced education, travel, and administration just kept opening to me. I had never dreamed of earning a PhD or writing books or directing a university department. I had envisioned my life as a stay-at-home wife and mother, keeping up my learning by helping my children with homework and reading in my spare time. *But if not?* My career required me to break ground at every step and tackle assignments for which I was not prepared. At the same time, it gifted me with incredible opportunities and interaction with scores of fascinating people.

I remember a student visiting me in my office after my first semester teaching religion at BYU. He thanked me for the class and then observed that I rarely spoke about myself in class. He cautiously asked me if I was married since I wore no ring and had never mentioned a husband. When I answered, "No, I am not married," he was surprised and blurted out, "But you're happy! I thought you couldn't be happy unless you were married!" My gratitude for valuable lessons gleaned through decades of being single is profound. With the Lord's enabling power, I learned to conquer fears, live independently, turn weaknesses into strengths, and find my voice. I learned to see "family" everywhere I worked and traveled and served.

I believe God had a different path for me than what I was capable of envisioning. I took the road less traveled. A road so much less traveled that I was the only one on it. Wait, that isn't true. I wasn't alone. It was on that road that I finally discovered the Lord—His matchless and limitless mercy, merits, and grace. It was on that road that I found myself in circumstances in which no one could help me but Him.

Along the way, amid trepidation and feelings that I didn't belong, I discovered abilities that I was certain I didn't have and successes in areas I didn't know existed. Marriage did eventually come to me, but it was on that road less traveled. My husband met me on my career path and supported me while walking beside me. Who would have thought that a first marriage at age forty-eight could be glorious? But it was and still is magical. On the road God prepared for me is where I found my greatest fulfillment and happiness. And greater meaning in many more areas of life than my teenage friends and I could have predicted when we graduated from high school.

The Book of Mormon prophet Nephi understood this divine phenomenon. He testified, "But the Lord knoweth all things from the beginning; wherefore, he prepareth a way to accomplish all his works among the children of men; for behold, he hath all power unto the fulfilling of all his words. And thus it is. Amen" (1 Nephi 9:6).

CHAPTER SEVEN
Our Response to the Unexpected

7

No matter what our age or circumstances in life, we can each bear witness to the disappointing reality of unfulfilled expectations. Whether it is due to misinformed interpretations of the Lord's promises, opposition in all things, or the natural consequences of living in a mortal body and personal agency—our own and others', we are living a reality that is different from what we anticipated. And we have survived. In truth, it is not our suffering, stumbling, and challenges that define us. Rather it is *how we respond* to them that determines our fulfillment and satisfaction in life. The choices we make and the attitudes we exhibit—after the unexpected happenings alter the details of our life—determine our happiness. Not what we might have been.

One reason for this reality is because success is slippery. We may feel great success today, but the euphoria dissipates tomorrow. Outward or extrinsic success is relative. Triumphs of power, fame, wealth, intellect, possessions, or influence are only measured in relation to the success others have achieved. Satisfaction with our outward achievements may then depend on how others perceive us. Or on how much we accomplish in comparison to others. Or in comparison to our earlier success. The more we obtain, the more we may expect to obtain. Extrinsic success demands constant feeding—through more praise, more increase, more power. More. More. More.

By contrast, intrinsic or inward success is almost always unexpected, remains in our memory, and continues to bring us joy long after the initial stimulus. Intrinsic accomplishments involve relationships—relationships with God, our Savior, our family, friends, neighbors, and even strangers at times. When we discover the value of inward success, we find that our list of expected outward successes diminishes and becomes simpler. Our happiness is not dependent on the praise and recognition of the world. We find satisfaction in helping others and in building relationships. If our deepest hope is to live as God invites us to live and as the Savior exemplified, we surrender expectations of obtaining more than others or garnering attention by our achievements. We forget about ourselves in our desire to serve others. When His apostles jostled with each other for

OUR RESPONSE TO THE UNEXPECTED

an elevated outward position, Jesus answered, "Whosoever will be great among you, let him be your minister; and whosoever will be chief among you, let him be your servant" (Matthew 20:26–27; see also Luke 22:24–27).

Ultimately, we not only want to become like our Savior, but we also desire an enduring and personal relationship with our Heavenly Parents and our Redeemer Jesus Christ. Even when it means sacrificing some of our expectations in mortality. President Russell M. Nelson witnessed, "Here is the grand truth: while the world insists that power, possessions, popularity, and pleasures of the flesh bring happiness, they do not! They cannot! What they do produce is nothing but a hollow substitute for 'the blessed and happy state of those [who] keep the commandments of God' [Mosiah 2:41]. The truth is that it is much *more exhausting* to seek happiness where you can *never* find it! However, when you yoke yourself to Jesus Christ and do the spiritual work required to overcome the world, He, and He alone, does have the power to lift you above the pull of this world."[1]

One of my favorite authors, often published in Church

magazines, was "Name Withheld." I loved their personal stories of dealing with serious challenges, of resilience, and finding hope when no hope seemed possible. I have frequently quoted from one such article written by Name Withheld, in which she told of her unexpected path to lasting happiness. "Sister Withheld" was in her forties, was a returned missionary, in good health, married to a faithful priesthood holder, mother to five outstanding children, and willingly serving in various Church callings. "Outwardly," she said, "I seem happy."

Initially, I thought this piece didn't fit the other articles Name Withheld authored. Where was the reason to protect identities? Then she told of her long battle with depression, of her hope for relief after consulting with professional therapists, and of her relapse to even lower levels of despair. Again, she went to her bishop to receive a referral to LDS Family Services. This time, her assigned therapist asked her to look him in the eyes and tell him that she knew who she was, had a testimony of her divine potential, and could feel Heavenly Father's love for her. She was shocked when she couldn't do it. The therapist told her that until she could feel a confirmation of her divine worth, she could not begin to heal.

Her therapist then gave her a personalized assignment to "find a time and place to be alone in nature and contemplate God's creations" and to take whatever time needed to receive confirmation of her intrinsic divine worth. Approaching the assignment "with such mixed feelings of fear, hope, skepticism, humility, sincere desire, and shaky faith," she opted to go to some beautiful mountains not far from where she lived. After a few hours, she noticed several sickly-looking pine trees leaning against much healthier ones. The longer she looked, the more she realized that if not for those healthy trees, the sickly ones would come crashing to the ground. She continued,

> As I contemplated those leaning trees, I came to understand that I had been very much like them. Because I lacked the inner strength that comes from self-respect, I had always leaned on other people for my self-worth by seeking approval from them. . . . As a result, I now felt as unhealthy emotionally and spiritually as those leaning trees looked physically.
>
> When people were not there to lend me strength, or when I perceived that they had in some way withdrawn their support, I came crashing down. I came to understand that instead of leaning on my fellow mortals for constant validations of my worth, I should be relying on the

foundation of my Father in Heaven and my Savior. They are constant. No matter how imperfect I am, they will always love me and be my source of strength. If I could learn to build my foundation on them, I could be strong and not so easily tossed to and fro like those bare, lifeless, leaning trees.

Wanting to ensure that she understood the lesson correctly, that she could change her life, and that this truth would permeate her heart, she prayed and received a witness of how much she was loved, especially by her Father in Heaven. From there she looked for ways to change. "The best way to learn [to love my family in a Christlike way] would be to serve them without expectations that they would validate my worth in return. As I listened and thought, I was filled with a Christlike love for my family, and I felt a peaceful, healing spirit flow over me. I knew my darkest hours were over."[2]

Sister Withheld's experience resonates with me. Her ability to articulate how she found healing that prevails beyond therapist appointments and recurring feelings of worthlessness echoes the outcomes promised from intrinsic success, building relationships, and selfless service. She illustrates through her personal healing the truths taught by our Savior and by President Nelson. I think Elder

OUR RESPONSE TO THE UNEXPECTED

Gary B. Sabin said it well when he testified that "when nothing is expected and everything is appreciated, life becomes magical."³ This is not to say that we should just toss out all our expectations. As was pointed out in the first chapter, expectations can be effective in propelling us to action, to dream and to stretch ourselves. Ultimately, however, our expectations can lead us to hope in Jesus Christ and to take on His yoke in place of our own (see Matthew 11:28–30). This process guides us to trust in the Lord's promises and timetable. It bolsters our faith to achieve unshakable confidence that "with God nothing [that He foresees in us] shall be impossible" (Luke 1:37). He will not fail us. Life becomes magical when we cease fixating on preconceived details of our expectations because our "hopes and fears of all the years"⁴ are met in the Holy One of Israel.

> Our expectations can lead us to hope in Jesus Christ and to take on His yoke in place of our own.

In conclusion, after exploring possible reasons why our expectations are derailed, we find that increased understanding of God's plan through study and lived experience repeatedly invites us to build our foundation on Jesus Christ. Because of hope in our Savior, joy, satisfaction, and even magic follow despair from unfulfilled expectations. Now consider with new eyes the following five verses from across the standard works. Do you find renewed hope for the future as you ponder these divine decrees?

- "[God] doeth not anything save it be for the benefit of the world" (2 Nephi 26:24).
- "Eye hath not seen, nor ear heard, neither have entered into the heart of man, the things which God hath prepared for them that love him" (1 Corinthians 2:9).
- "Believe in God; believe that he is, and that he created all things, both in heaven and in earth; believe that he has all wisdom, and all power, both in heaven and in earth; believe that man [and woman] doth not comprehend all the things which the Lord can comprehend" (Mosiah 4:9).
- "Ye cannot behold with your natural eyes, for the present time, the design of your God concerning those things which shall come hereafter, and the glory which shall follow after much tribulation" (Doctrine and Covenants 58:3).
- "What shall we then say to these things? If God be for us, who can be against us?" (Romans 8:31).

By pondering, connecting, and exploring scripture, we can't help but sense hope for whatever lies ahead. That hope is only available because of the mercy, merits, and

OUR RESPONSE TO THE UNEXPECTED

grace of the Holy Messiah. He alone can and will bring beauty from ashes—regardless of the bad breaks, unfairness, and others' agency that changed the details of our lives. Like the Apostle Paul, we can then "glory in tribulations." Why? Because we know "that tribulation worketh patience; and patience, experience; and experience, hope" (Romans 5:3–4). We try to see what lies ahead and make plans accordingly, *but if not,* He does. All He does is for our benefit, even if we can't decipher it now. Especially when immersed in our sorrows and heartache. In His wisdom, God created this world with invitations around every corner to learn to rely on Him, to grow in faith in Him—that with Jesus Christ, all things are possible.

This mortal life is a glorious adventure. It is full of surprises, both distressful and inviting. So, fasten your seat belt and expect the unexpected. The only constants in perfect love, complete understanding, and infinite enabling power are our Holy Father and His Beloved Son. Our living prophets and apostles will continue to lead us to Them. The holy scriptures will continue to educate our desires and expectations. So, what shall we do? Let us pursue truth, get back up after stumbling, seek opportunities to lift and serve others, and build relationships along the way. Day by day, year by year, we are learning to be more like Jesus. I'd call that exceeding expectations!

ACKNOWLEDGMENTS

I had not expected to write another book. It would not have happened except for the request and encouragement from trusted guides at Deseret Book. After presenting my speech at a Deseret Book event for "Questions Worth Asking," Laurel Christensen Day, Lisa Roper, and Celia Barnes each told me that I needed to make my remarks into a book. You were each so adamant and excited about the premise. Thank you all for seeing something in me that I thought was long gone.

But I needed regular encouragement and someone with whom I could bounce ideas around to even start writing again. My husband, Paul, has always been that brainstorming partner for me. Our brainstorming included exploratory discussions on vacation when I also had the fine minds of Rick and Marilyn Olson. They never disappointed with their ability to open whole new categories of thought and awareness,

I knew I needed some beta readers because the subject of unmet expectations can look so different for every person. Jan Heriford, Jayne Pulver, Holly Fronk, Celeste

ACKNOWLEDGMENTS

Mergens, and Kym Nelson answered in a big way. Each was sensitive to something different that I had missed and my wording in the book changed accordingly. My brother Hal Fronk was my best source of related quotes by great minds, in and out of the Church, for this book. Together these readers helped me craft a more inclusive manuscript.

Finally, I am indebted to the professional publishing team at Deseret Book. Janiece Johnson was more than an acquisitions director; she was a friend and confidant. And she gave me the best editor in Kristen Evans, an editor who seemed to know my intent instinctively and helped me communicate it in the best possible way. Many thanks to Rachael Ward as the typesetter and Heather Ward for designing the cover. They made me very happy. And a big shout-out to Rebecca Datwyler, who as product manager, took care of all the tiny details to grease the skids for publication.

Most of all, I acknowledge the grace and mercy of my Savior, who makes all of our righteous endeavors possible. With Him, I truly can do all that He calls me to do, even far beyond my natural abilities. If this little book succeeds in reaching your heart to grow your faith and hope for the future, it is because of the power and love of Jesus Christ.

NOTES

Chapter One: Unexpected Roadblocks

1. Jennifer Delgado, "Expectations: The Silent Killer of Happiness," *Psychology Spot*, https://psychology-spot.com/expectations-silent-killer-happiness; accessed 17 April 2024.

Chapter Two: Unfounded Interpretations of the Gospel

1. He is called "young" in Matthew 19:20, a "ruler" in Luke 18:18, and "rich" in Luke 18:23. He is described as having "great possessions" in Matthew 19:22 and Mark 10:22.
2. "Prosperity gospel," *Britannica*, https://www.britannica.com/topic/prosperity-gospel.
3. D. Todd Christofferson, "Our Relationship with God," *Liahona*, May 2022; emphasis added.
4. Christofferson, "Our Relationship with God."
5. Susan H. Porter, "Pray, He Is There," *Liahona*, May 2024.
6. *The Teachings of Spencer W. Kimball,* edited by Edward L. Kimball (Salt Lake City, UT: Bookcraft, 1982), 77; originally given in "Tragedy or Destiny" (Brigham Young University devotional, December 6, 1955); see also *Teachings of Presidents of the Church: Spencer W. Kimball,* 15.
7. Neal A. Maxwell, quoted in Bruce C. Hafen, *A Disciple's Life: The Biography of Neal A. Maxwell* (Salt Lake City, UT: Deseret Book, 2002), 20.
8. Dieter F. Uchtdorf, "*For the Strength of Youth*: The Savior's Message to You," *For the Strength of Youth*, March 2024.
9. *Lectures on Faith* (1985), 69.

NOTES

Chapter Three: Opposition in All Things

1. See "`itstsabown," Strong's Concordance of the Bible: 6089, 6093, https://www.biblestudytools.com/lexicons/hebrew/nas/itstsabown.html.
2. J. Richard Clarke, "The Value of Work," *Ensign*, May 1982.
3. Melinda Wheelwright Brown, *Eve and Adam: Discovering the Beautiful Balance* (Salt Lake City, UT: Deseret Book, 2020), 111.
4. Dieter F. Uchtdorf, "A Higher Joy," *Liahona*, May 2024.
5. Modification of Neal A. Maxwell, "Lest Ye Be Wearied and Faint in Your Minds," *Ensign*, May 1991, as seen in Jeffrey R. Holland, "Waiting on the Lord," *Liahona*, November 2020.
6. Francine R. Bennion, "A Latter-day Saint Theology of Suffering" (Brigham Young University Women's Conference, 28 March 1986); reprinted in *At the Pulpit: 185 Years of Discourses by Latter-day Saint Women,* Jennifer Reader and Kate Holbrook, eds. (Salt Lake City, UT: Church Historian's Press, 2017), 213–231.
7. Anne Morrow Lindbergh, *Gift from the Sea: Twentieth Anniversary Edition* (New York, NY: Vintage Books Edition, 1978), 108, 110.
8. Neal A. Maxwell, "Become Like God and Jesus Christ" (Ricks College devotional address, 16 October 1990).
9. Orianna Rosa Royle, "Nvidia Founder Tells Stanford Students Their High Expectations May Make It Hard for Them to Succeed," *Yahoo! Finance*, 13 March 2024, https://finance.yahoo.com/news/nvidia-founder-tells-stanford-students-121113900.html; originally featured in Fortune.com.
10. "Areopagitica: A Speech of Mr. John Milton for the Liberty of Unlicenc'd Printing, to the Parliament of England," *The John Milton Reading Room*, 1644.
11. Dale G. Renlund, "Choose You This Day," *Ensign*, November 2018.
12. Thomas S. Monson, "Joy in the Journey" (Brigham Young University Women's Conference, May 2008).

NOTES

Chapter Four: Our Bodies Are Mortal

1. Taylor G. Godoy, "Call, Don't Fall," *Liahona*, May 2024.
2. Dieter F. Uchtdorf, "Continue in Patience," *Ensign*, May 2010.
3. Boyd K. Packer, "The Word of Wisdom: The Principle and the Promises," *Ensign*, May 1996.
4. Russell M. Nelson, "Your Body: A Magnificent Gift to Cherish," *New Era*, August 2019.
5. Brook P. Hales, "Answers to Prayer," *Ensign*, May 2019.
6. Kate Bowler, *Everything Happens for a Reason: And Other Lies I've Loved* (New York, NY: Random House, 2018), 119–120, 170.
7. Bruce C. Hafen, *A Disciple's Life: The Biography of Neal A. Maxwell* (Salt Lake City, UT: Deseret Book, 2002), 16, 562.
8. Brent H. Nielson, "Is There No Balm in Gilead?", *Liahona*, November 2021.
9. As cited in Spencer W. Kimball, "Tragedy or Destiny" (Brigham Young University devotional, 6 December 1955), speeches.byu.edu; see also *Teachings of Presidents of the Church: Spencer W. Kimball*, 16.

Chapter Five: Agency vs. Expectations

1. Henry B. Eyring, "Do Not Delay," *Ensign*, November 1999.
2. Joseph Fielding Smith, *Doctrines of Salvation* 1:61; see also *Teachings of Presidents of the Church: Joseph Fielding Smith*, 293.
3. Frederik Hegner Odgaard, "Staying Strong When Loved Ones Leave the Church," *YA Weekly*, 7 April 2021.
4. Elder Brian K. Taylor explained, "We may not know the *why*, yet gratefully, we know He *who* loveth [us] and [doeth] all things for [our] welfare and happiness (1 Nephi 11:17; Helaman 12:2)" ("Swallowed Up in the Joy of Christ," *Liahona*, May 2024).
5. See Kylie Nielson Turley, *Alma 1–29: A Brief Theological Introduction* (Provo, UT: Neal A. Maxwell Institute, Brigham Young University, 2020): 87–94.

NOTES

6. As quoted in *The Teachings of Presidents of the Church: Spencer W. Kimball*, 16.
7. I am indebted to Janiece L. Johnson for this insight.
8. Dallin H. Oaks, "Opposition in All Things," *Ensign*, May 2016.
9. Jeffrey R. Holland, "Motions of a Hidden Fire," *Liahona*, May 2024.
10. "Does the Journey Seem Long?" *Hymns*, no. 127, verses 1 and 3.

Chapter Six: Divinely Designed Paths

1. D. Todd Christofferson, "Our Relationship with God," *Liahona*, May 2022.
2. Dieter F. Uchtdorf, "Continue in Patience," *Ensign*, May 2010.
3. Camille N. Johnson, "Invite Christ to Author Your Story," *Liahona*, November 2021.
4. Hugh B. Brown, "God Is the Gardener" (Brigham Young University commencement speech, 31 May 1968), speeches.byu.edu.
5. Brown, "God Is the Gardener."

Chapter Seven: Our Response to the Unexpected

1. Russell M. Nelson, "Overcome the World and Find Rest," *Liahona*, November 2022.
2. Name Withheld, "Learning to Rely on the Lord," *Ensign*, September 2003.
3. Gary B. Sabin, "Hallmarks of Happiness," *Liahona*, November 2023.
4. "O Little Town of Bethlehem," *Hymns,* no. 208.

ABOUT THE AUTHOR

Camille Fronk Olson is a professor emeritus of ancient scripture and former department chair at Brigham Young University. She received the Karl G. Maeser Excellence in Teaching Award, the university's highest recognition for teaching. She served a full-time mission to Toulouse, France, before earning a master's degree in ancient Near Eastern studies and a PhD in sociology of the Middle East. Formerly dean of students at LDS Business College, she has served on the Young Women General Board and on the Church's Teacher Development Curriculum Committee. Her published books include *In the Hands of the Potter*; *Mary, Martha, and Me*; *Too Much to Carry Alone*; *Women of the New Testament*; and *Women of the Old Testament*. She is married to Paul Olson, which includes the blessing of two children and four grandchildren.